# OUR TROUBLES IN POONA AND THE DECCAN

# OUR TROUBLES IN POONA AND THE DECCAN

BY

ARTHUR CRAWFORD, C.M.G.

GYAN

*Published by*

Gyan Publishing House
5, Ansari Road
Daryaganj, New Delhi-110002
Phone: 011-47034999, 9811692060
E-mail: books@gyanbooks.com

*Distribution Network*
gyanbooks.com
India, USA, Canada, UK, Australia



ISBN: 978-93-6208-268-8 (PB)
First Published, 1897

2nd Impression 2024

*Printed at:* Gyan Press, Delhi.



**OUR TROUBLES IN POONA AND THE DECCAN**
Author: ARTHUR CRAWFORD

# OUR TROUBLES IN POONA AND THE DECCAN.

THE FRIENDLY CONFERENCE.
SIWAJEE AND AFZOOL KHÁN, OCTOBER, 1659 A.D.
(*See page 110.*)

# OUR TROUBLES IN POONA AND THE DECCAN

BY

ARTHUR CRAWFORD, C.M.G.

Siwajee on the march.

WITH NUMEROUS ILLUSTRATIONS

BY

HORACE VAN RUITH.

---

WESTMINSTER
ARCHIBALD CONSTABLE & Co.
1897

# CONTENTS.

# SYLLABUS OF CONTENTS.

British Officers and Troops—Proposes to murder Elphinstone at a conference—Gôkhlà objects—The Dussera insult to British Troops, which change their position—An anxious night, 28 October—Gôklà urges action—Bájee Rao delays—More insults to Resident—The Battle of Kirkee—Signal defeat of Peishwa—Arrival of General Smith—He occupies Poona—Flight and pursuit of Bájee Rao—The Battle of Kôreygaum—Renewed flight of Bájee Rao, towards Mysore, back to Shôlapoor, to Chândore, to Kôpergaum, to Nágpoor territory—Is abandoned by all Chiefs except Vinchoorkur and Poorundharee—Appeals to Sir John Malcolm—Surrenders to Lieutenant Low, 3 June, 1818—Abdicates—Is pensioned at Bithoor—Adopts the future Náná Sahèb—End of the Bráhmin Dynasty—British accession—Bájee Rao's character—Elphinstone, Governor of Bombay—Thirty-seven years' peace—The Mutiny years—The Railway opened to Poona—Sir Bartle Frere—Prosperity of Poona—Its filthy condition—Its Riots, Dacoities, and Jubilee Murders—To whom ascribable—Inhabitants of Poona law-abiding—Only want governing—*Not* by Bráhmins.

## CHAPTER V.



Injustice of stigmatising all the Native Press as disloyal—Soundness of the Bombay Press—Faults of the Native Press—They exist in England—Good Anglo-Vernaculars—Congress newspapers—Their back-bone black-mail—"Sangvinary Veeds" thriving in high places, must be uprooted—The Law suffices—Temperature Chart of the Native Press.

## CHAPTER VI.



Saturday Street, Poona—The office of the "Scourge"—Bábá Sahèb—A sucking Peishwa—His ambition—The Pryvit Sahèb—How to start a Native Paper—The Editor's Room—A Brace of Rascals—The Secret Compact—The Babooneese language—Two Editorials in the "Scourge"—End of the Editor—The Snake's Progress—Bábá Sahèb's brilliant prospects.

## CHAPTER VII.



Curious outburst of Bráhmin patriotism—Valuable documents—Where Siwajee was burnt at Raighur—Siwajee's Durbars—Soyera Bye's Curse—View from Raighur—Áfzool Khán and Siwajee—Bráhmins arrange a friendly conference—Siwajee's religious and other preparations—The deadly embrace—Who would have thought it?—Killing no murder—Hurrah for Siwajee!

## CHAPTER VIII.

### THE INHABITANTS OF POONA.



Injustice of condemning all Bráhmins because there are some malignants—Good specimens—Judge Ránádè's admirable speech—The malign influence of the Deccan climate on Kônkanee Bráhmins—Swelled head—A specific for it—An unused Government remedy—Passionate Bráhmins prize fowls.

## CHAPTER IX.

### THE INHABITANTS OF POONA—*Continued.*



Deorookhas and Jáwala Bráhmins—Chitpâwans—Chiploon their place of origin—Why they are 'twice born'—The true Legend—Their Immortality—Their Treachery—Indra sees his mistake—Their little game—How Indra paid them out—Hurrah! they die like any Dèshast.

## CHAPTER X.

### THE INHABITANTS OF POONA—*Continued.*



Origin of the Shènwees—Shameful scandal spread by Chitpâwans—Shènwees are rivals to them—Their many good traits—Antidotes to Bráhmin poison—Perhaps the best of all Hindoos.

## CHAPTER XI.

### THE INHABITANTS OF POONA—*Continued.*



Their low position in the scheme of mixed castes—Another Bráhmin scandal—Their high character—Their tenderness to their women—Their conspicuous gallantry in battle—Three notable instances of it—Siwajee highly valued them—Their decay regrettable.

## CHAPTER XII.

### THE INHABITANTS OF POONA—*Continued.*



The habitat of the Syádree Máhráttás—Their warlike tradition—Are descended from Rájpoots—Wasteful cultivation—Their poverty and simplicity—Their mode of life—A terrible domestic tragedy—Father and Son—A grand old man—Ghâttees are descendants of Siwajee's Máwullees—How they have been gradually reclaimed and civilised—The Plain Máhráttás—The hereditary Patells or village head-men—Their good work—Their staunchness as soldiers.

## CHAPTER XIII.

### THE INHABITANTS OF POONA—*Continued.*



The Kônkanee Mussulman at home—Their good service after the Peishwa's downfall—Their deplorable decadence—The story of Abdul Farreed—He adopts a waif—Is tried for murder and acquitted—Throws up his appointment—Is pursued into his retreat by Bráhmin conspiracies—Is foully slandered about the waif Khatiza—Anonymous accusations—I visit him—He is persuaded to part with Khatiza, who marries—His persecution ceases.

## CHAPTER XVII.



The Mhárs are the aboriginals of Máháráshtra: are indispensable and ubiquitous: are splendid soldiers, good masons, good servants: shamefully neglected in Poona.

The Mhángs.—Their foul employment and food: their destitution: their extinction.

The Hill or Wild Tribes.—Rámooshees of the Ghauts—their bitter poverty: reasons for it: their evil traditions: they are used, cheated, and betrayed by Bráhmins: their presence in towns ominous: a Rámooshee Police Corps recommended.—Rámooshees of the Station are a mixed lot: their nocturnal and daily habits: their discretion.—Bheels, Kôlees, and Kátôdees do not come to Poona.

Brief list of Migratory and Predatory Tribes.—All filthy: all debauched—all thieves, except the Waddars, the Navvies of the Carnatic, who have been reclaimed.

The Tamásha Wallas or Showmen and Jugglers. Formerly accompanied Môgul armies: their honesty doubtful: they levy blackmail: their sudden disappearance from a city presages disturbance.

The Gôsáees have fought well in old days: are good spies: some are wealthy traders: the ascetics and contortionists probably half witted: Gôsáees needed in the Police.

## CHAPTER XVIII.



The Parsees.—Their worth: the superiority of their women: some distinguished Parsees: their benefactions: public spirit: enterprise: their services to the State: weak points of younger generation: exhortation to Parsees.

The Moodliars (Madrasses).—Their insignificance: are kindly, charitable easy-going, ready dupes: they represent nobody.

The Izrailies or Oil factors.—Their supposed origin: are good soldiers, mechanics and artificers.

Goanese and other Eurasians.—Are numerous: harmless, indolent: fond of liquor, poultry, and pork: good musicians: fair artificers: inherit weaknesses of both races.

## CHAPTER XIX.



Are utterly inefficient: sometimes brutal: are shamefully underpaid while heavily tempted.—Urgent need for reform.—Warnings from those who know disregarded.—Failure of Lord Harris's scheme.—Evil traditions of Poona Police: Two infamous Inspectors.—Reform very simple: how to be made: how to be paid for.

## CHAPTER XX.



General disaffection and discontent does *not* prevail in Máháráshtra—Is confined to a small body of one caste—Q.E.D.—The Moral—Hoping against Hope.

# LIST OF ILLUSTRATIONS

BY

HORACE VAN RUITH.

# LIST OF REFERENCES AND AUTHORITIES QUOTED.


HISTORY OF THE MAHRATTAS. (GRANT DUFF) *Times of India Press.*

INDIAN CASTE. (JOHN WILSON, D.D., F.R.S.) *Ditto.*

HISTORY OF THE PARSEES. (DOSSABHOY FRAMJEE KÁRAKA, C.S.I.) MACMILLAN & CO.

THE HINDU PANTHEON. (EDWARD MOOR). NEW EDITION WITH PLATES BY W. O. SIMPSON.

MEMOIR OF C. T. E. RHENIUS OF EDINBURGH. (BY HIS SON J. RHENIUS.)

MÁHÁBHÁRATA, MISCELLANEOUS EXTRACTS. (JOHN MUIR, D.C.L.)

MÁHÁBHÁRATA, FURTHER METRICAL TRANSLATIONS FROM THE. (JOHN MUIR, D.C.L.)

INDIAN AND ORIENTAL ARMS, ETC. (THE RIGHT HONBLE. LORD EGERTON OF TATTON.)

THE CONTEMPORARY REVIEW (JUNE 1897). ARTICLE BY MR. PATRICK GEDDES.

ONE HUNDRED BOMBAY NOTES. (EXTRACTS FROM DIFFERENT WRITERS.)

EARLY DAYS OF THE BHONSLAYS OF SÁTÁRA. (H. B. E. FRERE.)

# PREFACE.

"THE news from India is serious, though it must not be exaggerated. It does not follow that because English officers are shot at, the whole of India is in a state of latent rebellion," so said, wisely and temperately—as is its wont,—the *St. James's Gazette* of the 30th June after the Poona Jubilee murders. Would that the rest of the English Press had been as sober, as prudent! Alas! while the whole pack has been in full cry, Mahommedan fanaticism has been dragged, like red herrings tied to Bráhminical threads, across the scent. The pack has broken up. Some couples—the fiercest and the rashest—have run to heel on the line of Native Press Suppression; others have pursued the foul Plague phantom, and mauled brave "Tommy Atkins"; a few still bay at Bráhmins good and bad indifferently; while hare-brained Scotch, Irish, and "Padgett" M.P'S have ridden recklessly ahead, scattering on each line abundant lies, provided by cringing Fergusson College Professors and pestilent Deccan "Sabhás." "Filled is the air with barbarous dissonance" and the British public is bewildered.

There is great present danger that the innocent may be confounded with the guilty: there is greater danger that the guilty may evade detection—as has often happened before—and that the character of harmless classes may be irreparably injured through misapprehension. There is still greater danger that thus a general feeling of disaffection, which I hope to prove does not yet exist, may actually be produced.

At such a time it behoves those who have passed many years in Western India, who know something of the people and their languages, and who feel for their present sufferings from famine and pestilence, to endeavour to prevent the widening of the gulf that must always exist between Asiatics and their British rulers. If anything I have written, or may write, shall awaken keener interest in, diffuse a better knowledge of these peoples and of their real needs, I shall not have laboured in vain.

There are many books and documents bearing on the subject of this work, to which access has unfortunately been impossible because the India Office Library has been closed since June 1896. I have striven to make the best use of history, (quoting largely from Grant Duff,) of ancient Sanscrit traditions and legends, of the memoirs and researches of distinguished writers, and have ventured to intersperse incidents and experiences in my own life; thus bringing everything up to date, without, I hope, unfair comment, even on those misguided men—a mere handful, after all—who have brought about all the trouble.

The names of people and places are herein spelt in accordance with their rendering by Grant Duff and other Anglo-Indians before the Hunterian style was invented. Forced down officials' throats by official orders, the system has never been popular with the Services, nor has it ever been fully adopted.

Wherever Vernacular words or phrases have been used, the meaning or translation follows immediately for the enlightenment of the general reader.

ARTHUR CRAWFORD.

Dec. 1897.

# OUR TROUBLES IN POONA AND THE DECCAN.

## CHAPTER I.

### THE CITY OF POONA AND ITS ENVIRONS.

### Historical Sketch (1500 to 12th February, 1794).

#### Mállojee Bhônslay to Mhádájee Sindia.

THE capital of the Deccan was little more than a village in the 15th and 16th Centuries, owing its importance probably to the sanctity of the shrine of Parvatee (Parbuttee) or Bhowánee, built on the hill behind. Old Poona grew along the banks of the river Moota, from the tank at the foot of Parbuttee, and gradually extended over the plain to the East. Poona gave its name to the pergunnah (sub-district or county) which, with all the surrounding region, was subject to the Mahommedan Ahmednuggur Nizám-Sháhee (or Byheree) Dynasty. That dynasty fell into decay towards the end of the 16th Century when the Mahrattas were already becoming troublesome. Especially did the "respectable family" of the Bhônslays of Verole (Ellora) annoy their rulers. At last Mállojee Bhônslay, the grandfather of the great Siwajee, made himself such a nuisance that the Ahmednuggur Government to keep him quiet, granted him in 1604 the Pergunnahs of

Poona and Soopa in *Jagheer*, * handed him over the forts of Sewneree and Châkun and raised him to the command of 5,000 horse, with the title of Mállojee Rájá Bhônslay (Grant Duff, vol. 1, p. 78).

From that time the ancestors of Siwajee patronised the small Mahratta town, but it was not till after Siwajee's birth at Sewneree, in May 1627, that his father Sháhjee fixed upon Poona as the place where his son should be brought up. In 1637 he caused to be built a large "wárra" (Palace) for the residence of his wife Jeejeebye and young Siwajee, where the latter was educated (if education it can be called) under one Dádájee Kônedeo, the able Bráhmin who administered the revenues of that region and secretly encouraged his ward in all his warlike aspirations. We read little more about Poona till 1662, by which time Siwajee was in the height of his career. In this year Shaisteh Khán (Oomeer-ool Oomrah), Viceroy of the Deccan, was ordered by Aurungzebe to proceed from Aurungabad with a large force, to punish Siwajee for his daring incursions into Môgul territory. Shaisteh Khàn, marching by way of Ahmednuggur, easily took Poona which was then scarcely worth plundering, and thence, residing himself in the "wárra" or palace built for Jeejeebye, sent out detachments to take the Fort of Châkun, while Siwajee with his usual audacity made his headquarters at the Fort of Singurh, only eight miles off. Shaisteh Khán failing to dislodge Siwajee, "the mountain rat" (as Aurungzebe contemptuously called him), was super-

* Service tenure.

seded by Jèswant Sing, who being equally unsuccessful and greatly harassed by the Mahrattas, vacated Poona and returned to Aurungabad in 1663.

"During Shaisteh Khán's occupation Siwajee executed one of those daring exploits which so endeared him to his followers and which are still the themes of many a Mahratta bard.

"No armed Mahratta was permitted to enter Poona without a passport, and no Mahratta horsemen were entertained excepting under such chiefs * of their own as held their lands from the Emperor.

"Siwajee, watchful of all that passed, resolved to surprise the Khán, and sent two Bráhmins to make such arrangements as were necessary to gain admission. When his preparations were complete Siwajee left Singurh one evening in the month of April, a little after sunset, at the head of a considerable body of infantry, whom he posted in small parties along the road, but Yèsjee Kunk, Tánnajee Mâloosray, and 25 Máwulees were all that entered. His emissaries had gained a Mahratta foot-soldier in the Khán's service, who, on pretence of celebrating a marriage, obtained permission to beat through the town with the noisy instruments used on such occasions, and also for some of his companions, who always carry their arms, to join in the procession. Poona being an open town, Siwajee with his party, favoured by the contrivance of his emissaries, easily slipped undiscovered into the crowd, and joined in the moving assemblage.

* Khâfee Khan.

"When all was quiet, Siwajee and his companions, familiar with every accessible part of the Khán's residence, proceeded with a few pick-axes to the cook-room, above which there was a window slightly built up. Through this place they soon made themselves a passage, but not without alarming some of the women of the Khán's family, who immediately ran and awoke their master. Shaisteh Khán was hurrying out, and in the act of lowering himself from a window, when he received a blow on the hand which cut off one of his fingers. He was fortunate in escaping without further injury, as his son Abdool Futih Khán and most of the guard at his house were killed.

"Siwajee and his men retired before it was possible to intercept them, and gradually collected their parties on their route to Singurh. When they got to the distance of three or four miles they lighted torches, previously prepared, to occasion deception as to their numbers, and to express their defiance and derision. In this manner they ascended to the fort in full view of the Môgul camp from which they might be distinctly seen." (Grant Duff, pp. 164 to 166.)

Poona seems to have remained unmolested till 1685 when Khán Jehán, Môgul Viceroy, following up Siwajee's son Sumbhájee, (Siwajee died 5th April, 1680,) took possession of the town, now grown immensely, and all the adjacent country, which, however, was evacuated directly the Môguls entered on their Beejápur campaign.

The Plague is no new thing in Poona. In 1689 when Aurungzebe had conquered Beejápoor, a bubonic complaint, precisely resembling the plague now prevalent, broke out in his army, swept oft thousands of his troops and spread over the country, reaching Poona in 1690, where, however, having already spent its strength, it did not rage very violently. This epidemic had already been known for some years in the Deccan and Goozerat: "Khâfee Khan (the historian) describes it, as commencing by a slight swelling under the ear, the arm-pit or groin, attended with inflamed eyes and severe fever. It generally proved fatal in a few hours, and those who did recover, became wholly or partially deaf or blind." (Grant Duff, vol. 1, p. 333.)

From 1693 to 1699 Aurungzebe overawed the Deccan generally, and remained within striking distance of Poona (the name of which he changed to Môyàbad, from a grand cantonment which he built at Brimhapooree, on the Bheema, below Punderpoor). In 1699 the Emperor vacated this camp, to the great regret of the Môgul nobles, many of whom had built palaces there,—and marched past Poona to besiege the fort of Sátárá. For four or five years more the aged monarch, harassed on all sides by an unwieldy empire and exceptionally corrupt and debauched officers, many of whom while pretending to administer Mahratta Districts were receiving pay from their foes, "persevered to the last in his fruitless endeavours to stifle Mahratta independence." (Grant Duff, vol. 1, p. 339.) At last, in 1705, after having taken Rájgurh and Torna, and after camping in an aimless way for six months near Joonere, the Emperor left the vicinity of Poona for good, and retreated towards Beejápoor so as to check the spread of Mahratta disaffection in the Carnatic. Lastly the grand old man returned to Ahmednuggur, and on pitching his camp on the same spot which it had occupied with such splendour 21 years before, he predicted that "his end was near, his campaigns finished, his last earthly journey completed."

After his death (1707) the Mahratta nation began again to throw off the Môgul yoke, and would again have over-run all India but for the restraining influence of the Bráhmin Peishwas, who, absorbed in their ambitious projects of retaining all real power in their own hands, while they maintained a descendant of Siwajee as the nominal head of the nation, had no stomach for foreign aggression or the return of an era of rapine. From wise motives of policy as well as from inclination, they devoted much attention to the settlement of the country and the introduction of something like stable government. For this purpose they utilised two Mahratta chiefs who had come to the front during the long struggle with Aurungzebe, playing one against the other till they were nearly overwhelmed by both, when British power and influence restored their rule.

The Sindias, for example, claiming to be of Rájpoot descent, and with traditions as distinguished warriors in the Báhminee Dynasty, were connected by marriage with the Bhônslays (Siwajee's family, a daughter of the then Sindia, having been given in marriage to Shao, by Aurungzebe, about 1700). This man stuck to the Môguls, and was killed fighting under Azjim Sháh at the battle of Agra in 1707.

The family then fell into obscurity and even into poverty so abject that Ránojee Sindia, who afterwards restored its prestige, actually carried (so it is said) the Peishwa's slippers while he served in the Pâgah (or household troops) as a common trooper. Ránojee greatly distinguished himself in certain operations against the Soobadhar of Peishwa in 1724. Thenceforward his rise to great power was rapid. He died in 1750.

In this same campaign Mulharjee Hôlkar also came to the front. He was of low descent, a "dhangar" or shepherd of the village of Hôhl, of which his father was "Chowgula" or Deputy Patell. Mulharjee had already done good service with a small body of horse he had himself raised. These two rival powers alternately occupied the city and its environs for thirty years; it was during their time that Poona began to be studded with huge semi-fortified "wárras" or Palaces built by the various Sirdars of the Deccan, each anxious to assert his position in the town which Ballajee Bájee Rao Peishwa proclaimed in 1750 to be "Capital of the Mahrattas."

Mahommedan power, however, was not yet by any means completely humbled. It was now Hyderabad that threatened Máhárâshtra, and the short but sharp struggle that followed was complicated by the French successes under Bussy,—with which I need not concern myself, seeing that that nation never reached the city of Poona, and that its hard-won possessions in the Deccan were practically lost after Bállajee Bájee Rao's operations against Nizám Ály in 1756.

Nizám Álly, appointed by his brother Sulábhut Jung to be Governor of Berar, conceived the audacious plot, to which Bállajee Bájee Rao was doubtless privy, to intern Sulábhut Jung in Dowlutabad, assume the reins of power and to expel the French from the Deccan. In the general scrimmage that followed, the Bráhmin Peishwa had fine opportunities of indulging his passion for intrigue. He set the Mahrattas plundering under Vishwásrao and others, while he pompously made friends with Nizám Álly: he paid court to Bussy directly he appeared on the scene to Sulábhut Khan's aid with a strong force of European cavalry and infantry: he humbled himself to Hyder Jung and did all he could (but in vain) to induce Bussy to give him Dowlutabad. Finally, he left his quondam friend Nizám Álly in the lurch, and in June 1750, withdrew with his whole army to Poona, employing his leisure in fooling the Bombay Government (Mr. Bourchier and Mr. Ellis) about Surat (March 4th, 1759).

Nizám Ally was not the sort of man to forgive or forget such treachery. No sooner had Bussy left for Pondicherry than Nizám Ally reappeared stronger than ever at Boorhánpoor, and, Sulábhut Khán joining him, marched for Poona. Bállajee Bájee Rao in person moved out with a large force to Ahmednuggur to meet him, while Sewdáseo Rao went eastward, encountered and signally defeated the two brothers (Nizám and Sulábhut) near Oordgeer, and forced them to conclude a treaty (1760) by which the Môgul possessions in the Deccan were now confined to

PARBUTTEE TEMPLE AND PALACE.
SHOWING KIRKEE BATTLEFIELD AND SITE OF LATE JUBILEE MURDERS.
(*See pages 64—68, 98 and 229*).

an insulated space, which must, it seemed, be soon overwhelmed. (Grant Duff, vol. 1, p. 594.) But Nizám Álly in 1763 seized the first opportunity, and evading the two Hôlkars (Dummajee and Mulharjee), who tried to stop him, marched straight on Poona, which he plundered and burnt, pulling down such "wárras" as were not ransomed. The people of Poona at the first alarm skedaddled with as much as they could carry to Singurh and the hill forts of the Kônkan, but the pursuit was so rapid that many were overtaken and "many manuscripts and state papers illustrative of Mahratta history were totally destroyed." (Grant Duff, vol. 1, p. 635.) Nizám Álly then withdrew to Aurungabad for the rainy season, whence he soon moved out to join the defeated Môgul army from Hyderabad, which was then being closely pursued by Rugonâth Rao. A great battle ensued at Rakisbone on the Gôdávery, at which Nizám Álly, on the wrong side of the river, had the mortification of seeing the flower of his army cut to pieces without being able to succour them; he retreated with the remnants of his band to Aurungabad where the Mahrattas pursued and again attacked him. Nizám Álly then saw the error of his ways, visited Rugonâth Rao, and induced that good-natured man to give him 10 lakhs of rupees and to conclude a new treaty with him (October 1763). With Nizám Álly's further career and his treaty with the English on the 12th October, 1800, the city of Poona has but little concern. He died at Hyderabad in August 1803.

In the meantime the Peishwas had their work cut out

at Poona by the two great Mahratta rivals whom they had raised to power. Mhádájee Sindia, the greatest Mahratta diplomatist and the best administrator the nation ever had, from the outset of his career undoubtedly had secret intentions of allying himself with the English, and the Governor-General, Warren Hastings, as well as Mr. Hornby, Governor of Bombay, were disposed to meet him half way, but Sindia played, as usual, a double game and would not declare himself (1778). So matters drifted, and Hôlkar, ingratiating himself with Náná Furnáwees—always the opponent of British influence,—became the chief power at Poona for a time. Had Mhádájee Sindia acted openly, history might have read another way, for "certain it is that he had in view the control of the Bráhmins and the establishment of his own authority at the Peishwa's Capital." (Grant Duff, vol. 2, p. 251.) With characteristic duplicity, however, he obtained from the Emperor of Delhi "patents constituting the Peishwa "Wakeel-i-Mootluq" (or chief agent) of the Deccan, but which was now to descend to him as a hereditary office in unalienable "*enam*," * on condition, however, of his appointing Sindia and his posterity his perpetual deputies." Once at Poona Mhádájee thought to suppress the Bráhmins; whether he would then have been content to remain as Prime Minister of the Rájá of Sátárá, descendant of Siwajee and nominally head of the Mahratta nation, or whether he would have fixed himself as the Ruler of the Empire—who can tell?

* Hereditary gift.

Mhádájee Sindia's duplicity defeated itself. Armed with these patents he set out on a long and pompous march to Poona, which is still spoken of with awe and admiration and many "Wáh! Wáhs!" under many a village Peepul tree from Burhánpoor to Ahmednuggur. On the way he dallied with Nizám Álly, and pretended to be much hurt because the latter would not give him the fertile district of Bheer and bestow Aurungabad on the Peishwa! This potentate, or rather Náná Furnáwees, alarmed at his approach sought aid from Lord Cornwallis, who, however, declined to interfere even though Náná offered to subsidise and permanently maintain a detachment of regular troops under a British officer. Arrived near Poona, however, Sindia, to allay Náná's fears, left his main army behind, and with only a few Europeans under Hessing, an Englishman, and one regular battalion commanded by Filoze the Neapolitan, encamped on the 11th June, 1791, at the junction (known by us as the "Sungum") of the Moota and Moolla rivers.

Náná Furnáwees did all he knew for 9 days to prevent the young Peishwa from accepting the patents and decorations from the Emperor of Delhi, brought by Sindia, but the latter persisted, so Náná was compelled much against the grain to pay a formal visit to Sindia, who received him with great outward show of respect and humility. Next day Sindia was admitted to an audience with the Peishwa whom he endeavoured to conciliate "with numberless rare productions and curiosities from Hindostan." On the following morning took place the grand ceremony of investing the Peishwa with the title and dignity of "Wakeel-i-Mootluq." Splendid "Shamiánas" or Durbar tents were pitched, at the end of which was a throne on which lay the Imperial "firmaun" or patent, the dresses of honour and the decorations. Advancing up the Durbar, the Peishwa thrice saluting the throne, deposited on it his "nuzur" of 101 gold mohurs, and seated himself at the left of the throne; the Imperial firmauns were then read, including one which forbade the slaughter of bullocks and cows. The Peishwa then received the "khillut" or presents, and retiring into a small tent, arrayed himself in the dresses of honour, returned and re-seated himself, whereupon Sindia, Náná Furnávees and other subordinate officers presented their "nuzurs" to him in congratulation.

The Peishwa then rose, seated himself in the state "nalkee" or sedan chair just received, and was carried in great pomp to the city of Poona, followed and fanned by Sindia. Arrived at the Peishwa's Palace, the ceremony of investing Sindia with the Deputyship was duly performed. But on this occasion, as on many others, Sindia overdid his humility, when he begged to be regarded only as a hereditary servant of the Peishwa "entitled only to carry his slippers" and to be addressed merely as "Patell." This affectation, intended to please and deceive the Bráhmins, did neither, while it disgusted and enraged Sindia's Mahratta followers who had already refused to enter the Imperial Durbar tents, or to present "nuzurs" to the Peishwa as "Mooktyar-i-Mootluq". However, Sindia, with the frank *bon-*

*hommie* he knew so well to put on, soon found favour with the Peishwa Mhadow Rao, was his constant companion in hawking and other field sports, and lost no opportunity of trying to undermine the influence of Náná Furnávees, hinting that he was both able and willing to release the young Peishwa from Náná's irksome control. For a time Sindia made little progress, but an imprudence of Náná's giving Sindia an excuse for bringing to Poona another Infantry Brigade, under M. Perron, and increasing the Europeans under Hessing and Filoze, Náná was overawed and Mhádájee Sindia loomed all-powerful in the eyes of Hindostan and in the mind of the young Peishwa.

"Sindia became all-powerful in Hindostan, but was conscious of his unpopularity in the Deccan, and strove to overcome it. With this view he had, on his arrival at Poona, espoused the cause of the Gaekwár of Baroda, and upon one occasion, when Náná Furnáwees, during the minority of the Punt Suchew, assumed charge of his lands, Sindia, who knew that the proceeding met with general disapprobation, interposed, conveyed the Suchew to Poona, in opposition to to the orders of the minister, re-established him in his possessions, and dismissed the agent whom Náná had placed in charge of the Suchew's territory. This daring interference gave rise to a quarrel, which was with difficulty appeased; but fresh disputes arose in consequence of Sindia's more undisguised attempts to induce the young Peishwa to seek his protection. On one occasion, in particular, a conversation took place in a boat at Lôhgaom, which, being overheard and repeated, caused such alarm in the mind of Náná, that he took the first opportunity of coming to an explanation with the Peishwa.

"He addressed himself both to the youth's judgment and feelings; enumerated the services he had performed for him and for the State; described the views of aggrandisement entertained by Sindia; pointed to his foreign troops, his departure from ancient usage, and his want of connection with the Mahratta people, over whom and the Bráhmin sovereignty he was bent on establishing an absolute power. With these observations he contrasted his own situation, his inability to preserve order or to resist the encroachments of Sindia if unsupported by his own prince; and finally, lamenting in tears the probable effects of the evil counsels by which the latter had been misled, he tendered his resignation and declared his resolution to proceed to Benâres. Young Mhádow Rao was greatly affected. In a transport of grief he begged Náná's forgiveness, entreated him to stay, and promised to be for ever guarded in his conduct. But notwithstanding this re-establishment of Náná's personal influence and the friendship for him of the powerful Bráhmin families and the old "mánkurees" or great men, Mhádájee Sindia would undoubtedly have prevailed, but in the midst of his ambitious schemes he was suddenly seized with violent fever which in a few days terminated his existence. He breathed his last at Wunowree, in the environs of Poona, on the 12th February, 1794." (Grant Duff.)

Thus passed away the only Mahratta Chief who ever seriously set himself, who ever possessed the power, to emancipate his nation from Bráhminical thraldom; who failed because he would not trust the sword by which he had won his way upward, because he would not be honest and frank with his own people, because he thought to beat Bráhmins with their own peculiar weapons of intrigue, deceit and bluster. "In his progress he first assisted one Bráhmin against the other, and then attempted to overawe him whom he had raised." He was nearly as well educated as any Bráhmin of his day—he wrote well, spoke well, and was a good accountant; his own kingdom in Málwa was the best managed in Hindostan; circumstances were all in his favour, especially at the end of his career—but great as was his political sagacity he was ever led astray by a violent temper, by revengeful feelings, by ambition, by distrust of those whom he should have trusted. Had Mhádájee Sindia refrained from quarrelling with Hôlkar; had he combined with the Gaekwár, the Powárs, the Bhônslay of Nágpoor; had he possessed the moral courage to ally himself with the English in 1792—to declare himself the champion of "Máháráshtra for the Mahrattas": a descendant of the house of Siwajee Bhônslay might even now be reigning in the capital of the Deccan.

# CHAPTER II.

## Historical Sketch—*Continued.* (1794 to 1799.)

Suicide of the Peishwa—Plot against Bájee Rao.—Deposition of Bájee Rao.—Resignation of Náná Furnáwees.—Restoration of Bájee Rao.—Náná again triumphant.

MHÁDAJEE Sindia's death of course brought the Bráhmins again to the front, and Náná Furnáwees rose to the zenith of his power. His restraint of the young Peishwa Mhádow Rao, though he was 26 years of age (1795), so far from relaxing became more rigid, till Mhádow Rao, goaded to madness by the insidious messages of his cousin Bájee Rao, lost his head, was seized with melancholia, and at last (25th Oct., 1795) committed suicide by throwing himself from a terrace of his palace in Poona.

Frightfully injured, the unfortunate young man lingered for two days and expired in the arms of Bábá Rao Phurkay (or Phudkay), expressly enjoining that his cousin Bájee Rao should succeed him. "This tragedy was an event of awful importance to the political existence of Náná Furnáwees."—Before the breath was out of Mhádow Rao's body, Náná summoned Purèshram Bhow to Poona "with every man he could collect", and the day after the funeral obsequies, Rughoojee Bhônslay and Dowlut Rao Sindia were recalled to

SUMBHAJEE'S DAY DURBAR AT RAIGURH.—THE CURSE OF SOYERA BYE, 1680 A.D.

(*See page 106.*)

confer with Náná and Tookajee Hôlkar who was then resident in Poona. Even from them Náná Furnáwees carefully withheld poor Mhádow Rao's dying injunction regarding Bájee Rao, whom he represented as the incarnation of evil, and intimately connected with the English. Hôlkar and the other chiefs concurring in these views, Náná unfolded his plan, which was simple enough. Yessowda Bye, widow of the suicide, was to adopt a son who should succeed as Peishwa, Náná continuing to govern in his name. Hôlkar and all the principal chiefs, except Bálloba Tattya on behalf of Dowlut Rao Sindia, gave their consent in writing and withdrew from Poona (January 1796); Tookajee Hôlkar, however, remained behind to back up Náná if occasion should arise. The Bombay Government, informed through Mr. Mostyn (recently appointed first Resident at Poona) of the arrangement, saw no reason to interfere. Náná Furnáwees' intrigue thus seemed likely to succeed at every point.

But Náná, much as he feared, and closely as he watched Bájee Rao, was no match for that astute young gentleman, who was regularly informed of all that occurred, and entered into correspondence with Bálloba Tattya. Having gained over this minister, Bájee Rao "addressed himself next to Dowlut Rao Sindia, offering him four lakhs of territory and whatever might be the expense of his troops during the time he should require their aid in asserting his lawful succession to the Musnud (throne)." Dowlut Rao Sindia accepted the offer with alacrity, and a formal agreement was drawn up, the ink of which was scarcely dry before its contents were communicated to Náná Furnávees. Scared out of his wits, he summoned Purèshram Bhow and they twain concluded that discretion was the better part of valour, that it would be best "to anticipate Sindia's design to release Bájee Rao, and to declare him Peishwa." So Purèshram Bhow hied him to the Fort of Sewneree where Bájee Rao was interned—the latter, tolerably sure of Sindia's sticking to his agreement, was not in violent haste to accept the Peishwaship thus offered—he insisted upon many guarantees, indeed it was not till he had compelled Purèshram Bhow "to hold on by the tail of a cow and swear by the holy Gôdávery that *no* deception was intended" that he would leave the Fort. Arrived at Poona, Náná Furnáwees immediately waited on him—when the two arch rascals agreed to bury the hatchet in formal documents. That given by Bájee Rao to Náná ran as follows—I have not traced the other.

"In the presence of my God, and from the inmost recesses of my heart, have I rooted out every vestige of any former act; let all your future conduct be guided by the principles of good faith. I will never injure you or yours, by word or deed, by any inward thought or outward act, neither will I allow any other person to do so; so on this point I will be inflexible, and will pay no attention to the suggestions of others. I will not allow your reputation to be sullied, and should any one attempt to instil anything of the kind into my breast, I will point him out to you. I will never release any one from confinement without your advice: all state affairs shall be managed by our conjunct council. From this day all your acts are mine: suspicion is wholly eradicated from my heart."

The incidents of 1796 show how these solemn compacts were observed, and are illustrative alike of Mahratta and Bráhmin character. They are so well related by Grant Duff, that I cannot do better than quote from him, making a few alterations, and omitting certain paragraphs which do not concern Poona, or which introduce persons who are not essential to the Poona narrative.

"Bálloba Tattya, on hearing of the step which Bájee Rao had taken, was incensed at his conduct, but determined to counteract the schemes of Náná Furnáwees. He therefore persuaded Sindia, then on the banks of the Gôdávery, to march on Poona with his whole force. Náná Furnáwees was dismayed; Purèshram Bhow advised him to stand firm, to collect the troops, and to give battle; but Náná, deficient in personal courage, was also sensible of the superiority of Sindia's army; he could not trust Bájee Rao, and he was terrified lest he should fall a prisoner into the hands of Bálloba Tattya, by whom he believed he would be put to death. Having therefore left Purèshram Bhow with Bájee Rao at Poona, he told the latter that as Sindia was advancing with intentions hostile only towards himself, he thought the best means of averting ruinous civil dissensions was for himself to retire from business, and withdraw from the capital. He accordingly repaired first to Poorundhur, and afterwards to Sátára. Sindia arrived in the neighbourhood of Poona, and had a friendly interview with Bájee Rao; but Bálloba Tattya, although he affected to meet him with cordiality, could not forget Bájee Rao's behaviour. After considering various plans, Bálloba Tattya at last resolved to set aside Bájee Rao, and to raise both a minister and a Peishwa of his own; for which purpose he proposed to Purèshram Bhow, that Mhádow Rao's widow should adopt Chimnajee Appa * as her son, that Bájee Rao should be placed in confinement, and that Purèshram Bhow should conduct the administration. Purèshram Bhow had begun to despise Náná Furnawees for his pusillanimous conduct, but he still so far respected his wisdom as to ask his opinion. Náná advised him to accept what was proposed, but to take care that Bájee Rao came into his own custody.

"To this last essential part of the advice no attention was paid by Purèshram Bhow. Bálloba Tattya pretended to be partly influenced in the measure he now pursued, by the hope of rendering it, in some degree, acceptable to Náná Furnáwees, lest the latter, in the present state of Dowlut Rao Sindia's inexperience, should form some confederacy, by means of other chiefs, against the house of Sindia. Bálloba accordingly, as soon as Náná's assent had been obtained, made overtures for a reconciliation, to which the latter made no objections.

"Náná's own proceedings in the meantime deserve notice. When he quitted Poorundhur and repaired to Sátára, he

* A brother of Bájee Rao.

entertained some design of emancipating the puppet Rájá, and restoring the old form of the government of Siwajee, as a plan calculated to avert the dissensions that had arisen, which were likely to increase in the state; but a very few days convinced him of the futility of this scheme. Rám Rájá, the puppet, in consequence of the treatment he had experienced, had no confidence in him. The Rájá's name was sufficiently popular to have brought many of the most warlike Mahratta families to his standard, and to have awakened a powerful interest amongst the descendants of the first followers of Siwajee, residing in the wilds of the Máwuls and Khôras. Rám Rájá, though incapable of conducting state affairs himself, was a man of courage, and several of his relations were fit leaders for any desperate enterprise. But Náná's object was to control the chiefs of the empire, not to stir up a power subversive of all order. After a few conferences therefore he desisted, and retired to Waee, a town in the neighbourhood; but his having entertained such a scheme was so far fortunate for the Rájá, that he was indulged in a little more liberty, and treated with greater kindness and consideration.

"When Náná Furnáwees consented to the proposal of Bálloba Tattya for adopting Chimnajee Appa, it became necessary as a matter of form to obtain the Rájá's 'khillut', so he promised that, if he ever had an opportunity, he would endeavour to fulfil the agreement made with Rám Rájá in the time of Bállajee Bájee Rao, by putting Rájá Shao in possession of the territory promised by the treaty of Sàngola.

"Náná would have proceeded to Poona, but on finding that Purèshram Bhow had allowed Sindia's minister to retain the person of Bájee Rao, he suspected, and with good reason, that the whole was a scheme to entice him into the power of Bálloba Tattya; and, therefore, although he forwarded the 'khillut,' he himself remained at Waee.

"Bájee Rao was still ignorant of the plot that had been formed against him, and the manner of disclosing it is too characteristic, not only of Bráhmins, but of the future ways of the Poona court, to be omitted. Some demands for money on account of Sindia's expenses were made on Bájee Rao, and, upon his expressing inability to comply with them, they were urged in a tone which produced altercation, and Sindia, pretending to take offence at the manner of Bájee Rao's refusal, begged permission to return to Hindostan. Bájee Rao, as had been foreseen, immediately repaired to Sindia's camp for the purpose of privately expostulating; he was there detained in argument until late in the evening, when the conference was suddenly interrupted by intelligence of Purèshram Bhow's having carried off Chimnajee Appa; no one, it was pretended, knew whither, but it was supposed to Sátára. Bájee Rao, alarmed and astonished, begged of Sindia to pursue them; but the uncertainty of their route, the strength of their party, and the darkness of the night were urged against this proposal. A request, however, to be allowed to continue under Sindia's protection during the night was readily granted, and next day he discovered the snare, being advised to remain, 'as any place beyond the precincts of Sindia's camp was unsafe for his highness.'

"In the meantime Purèshram Bhow had merely conveyed Chimnajee Appa into the city of Poona; but Chimnajee positively refused to become a party to the unjust usurpation of his brother's rights, and compulsion only induced him to bear his share in it.

"He was adopted by the name of Chimnajee Mhádow, and formally invested as Peishwa on the 26th May.

"The day after the installation of the new Peishwa, Purèshram Bhow proposed that Náná Furnàwees should come to Poona, meet and be reconciled to Bálloba Tattya, and afterwards assume the civil administration in the New Peishwa's government, whilst the command of the troops and all military arrangements should remain with himself. In reply to this proposal, Náná Furnáwees requested that Purèshram Bhow's eldest son, Hurry Punt, might be sent to Waee for the purpose of clearly settling some preliminaries; but instead of coming as an envoy, Hurry Punt crossed the Neera at the head of 4,000 or 5,000 chosen horse, a circumstance that in itself naturally excited Náná's suspicions, which were strengthened by the receipt of a secret letter, advising him to seek his own safety without a moment's delay.

"The fortunes of Náná Furnáwees were now, in the general opinion, and perhaps in his own, desperate; but on being forced to abandon half-measures, into which he was misled by a timid disposition, the vigour of his judgment, the fertility of his expedients, the extent of his influence, and the combination of instruments which he called into action surprised all India, and, from his European contemporaries, procured for him the name of 'the Mahratta Machiavel.'

"When he saw the danger imminent, he immediately fled from Waee towards the Kônkan, blocked up the passes in his rear, threw a strong garrison into Pertabgurh, and, on arriving at the village of Mhár, his first care was to put the fort of Raigurh in the best state of defence. Bálloba Tattya proposed that he should be followed up without delay, and offered some of Sindia's regular infantry for the purpose; but Purèshram Bhow, influenced by secret well-wishers of Náná, objected to the employment of coercive measures, although his hostility was soon after avowed by his giving up Náná's 'jágheer' lands to Sindia, and sequestrating his houses and property in Poona for his own use.

"The revolution above sketched naturally tended to unite Bájee Rao and Náná Furnáwees; and a secret intercourse was carried on between them, through the medium of a Mahratta Sillidar, named Bállajee Koonjur, who visited Náná Furnáwees at Mhár, and conveyed the most friendly declarations and assurances on the part of Bájee Rao, while begging Náná to exert himself in their mutual behalf.

"Náná Furnáwees, however, already had every engine at work. Bábá Rao Phurkay, in command of the Peishwa's household troops, had engaged to bring them over to him. Tookajee Hôlkar's whole power and influence were ready at his signal, and Náná had opened a negotiation with Sindia, offering to him the Putwurdhun 'jágheer' and the fort of Ahmednuggur with territory yielding 10 lakhs of rupees, on condition that he would place Bálloba Tattya in confinement, re-establish Bájee Rao on the 'musnud', and return with his army to Hindostan.

"Thus far of his plans Náná Furnáwees communicated to Bállajee Koonjur for Bájee Rao's information.

"By the aid of Sakaram Ghátgay of Kâgul, Náná Furnàwees was successful in gaining over Sindia to his cause, and the party became less circumspect in their preparations. Bájee Rao in the midst of Sindia's camp, assisted by his father's friend, the veteran Mánájee Phakray, used supplies of money furnished by Náná Furnáwees, in levying troops.

"These imprudent proceedings were discovered by Bálloba Tattya, who seized some of the leaders and attacked two others, Neelkunt Rao Purbhoo and Mállojee Ghôrepuray. They had but a few minutes to prepare for defence, but they repulsed the troops sent to apprehend them, and, at the head of a few followers, made good their retreat from Poona to the strong range of hills south of the Neera.

"Bájee Rao's place of encampment within Sindia's lines was then surrounded and the water-supply cut off. The troops he had assembled were permitted to disperse, but Mánájee Phakray enjoined them to meet him in the neighbourhood of Waee, where they assembled accordingly, and were, promptly joined by Neelkunt Rao and Mállojee

Ghôrepuray, Náná Furnáwees supplied them with money, directed them to take up a position at the Sálpee Ghaut, where they soon collected 10,000 men, and declared for Bájee Rao.

"Bálloba Tattya, unconscious of the inextricable and extensive toils which Náná was weaving around him, attributed the whole plot to Bájee Rao, and therefore determined to send him off a prisoner to Hindostan.

"He was despatched, accordingly, under the care of Sakaram Ghátgay, to whom the command of his escort was entrusted. But Bájee Rao, aware of the most likely means of gaining Sindia, employed all his eloquence to induce Ghátgay to give his beautiful daughter to Sindia in marriage, on condition of Bájee Rao's being elevated to the throne. At last, pretending to be won over, Ghátgay agreed to give his daughter on the following conditions: that Bájee Rao should authorise him to promise Sindia two crores of rupees in ready money on his becoming Peishwa; that, when Peishwa, he should get him (Ghátgay) appointed Sindia's prime minister; and that he should also endeavour to obtain for him the village of Kâgul in 'enam'. Having assented to these conditions, Bájee Rao feigned sickness, and Ghátgay remained with him on the banks of the Paira.

"At Poona great preparations were going forward. Hôlkar's and Sindia's troops were held in readiness apparently to oppose Bájee Rao and Náná Furnáwees, and after the Dussera, which happened on the 11th October, the regular battalions in the Peishwa's service under Mr. Boyd marched to the Neera bridge, and a brigade of Sindia's regulars proceeded towards Raigurh. These movements were made by Purèshram Bhow himself, or artfully suggested by some conspirators, in order to veil the deception about to be practised on Bálloba Tattya.

"The schemes of Náná Furnáwees were now matured. In addition to what has been explained, he had incited the Rájá of Kôlapoor to attack the districts of Purèshram Bhow; he had obtained Nizám Álly's approbation of the draft of a treaty, afterwards settled on the 8th October, with Musheer-ool-Moolk, the basis of which was to be the re-establishment of Bájee Rao on the 'musnud,' and his own re-establishment as minister; for which the territory ceded to the Peishwa by a former convention was to be restored, and the balance of the stipulated money-payment remitted.

"A negotiation with Rughoojee Bhônslay had been equally successful.

"To him Náná promised 15 lakhs of rupees for his immediate expenses, the district of Mundelah, and the fort of Chooreeágurh with its dependencies. Three thousand horse which, by treaty, he was bound to furnish when required, were now only to be called for on emergencies. Some other advantages were also held out, and Rughoojee had solemnly promised his support.

"The principal powers having been thus secured, the English having also expressed their approbation of Bájee Rao's being elevated to the 'musnud,' Sindia on the 27th October, arrested Bálloba Tattya, and sent a body of his troops, to seize Purèshram Bhow, but the latter was warned through a note brought to him in mistake for Puréshram Bhow Putwurdun. Instantly on reading it, he got ready a body of horse, and taking Chimnajee Appa with him, fled with precipitation to Sewneree; but he was quickly pursued, and compelled to surrender.

"Bájee Rao was now brought back in triumph, and encamped at Korygaom, on the Beema, 18 miles from Poona.

"Náná Furnáwees having joined his own army at the Sálpee Ghaut, the infantry under Mr. Boyd having likewise placed themselves under his orders, he commenced his march for the capital. But on the route, having received a note from Bájee Rao which hinted at the tardiness of his proceedings, he took alarm, and before he would advance, insisted upon receiving a written declaration from Bájee Rao that he intended no treachery towards him, and that, in case of desiring to resign his situation as minister, he should be permitted to retire where his person and property would be secure. A treaty of guarantee was at the same time entered into by Nizám Álly and Sindia, agreeing to establish Bájee Rao on the 'musnud,' and to reinstate Náná Furnáwees as prime minister; but they also, with a view of securing themselves, agreed to force Náná to fulfil the articles of the respective treaties which he had made with them.

"These preliminaries being adjusted, Náná Furnáwees returned to Poona, and resumed the duties of prime minister on the 25th November. The insignia of investiture having been procured from Sátára, Bájee Rao was at last seated on the 'musnud', 4th December, 1796. It was declared by a council of Shâstrees that the relationship between the late Peishwa, Mhádow Rao Narrain, and the sons of Rugonath Rao, prevented the widow of the former from adopting the second cousin of his father; the adoption of Chimnajee Appa was therefore declared illegal, and annulled; the Shâstrees who had performed the ceremony were expelled, and Chimnajee Appa, though he had acted on compulsion, was obliged to undergo penance to atone for the deed, but was shortly after appointed by his brother to the government of Guzerát."

It is impossible in a mere historical sketch of Poona such as this is, to dwell in detail on the stirring events, the multitudinous intrigues and counter-intrigues, the incessant treacheries, by which each party—Bráhmin and Mahratta—Peishwa and Prime Minister—Sindia and Hôlkar pursued their ends between 1797 and 1817, when the power of each and all was destined to be shattered by the steadfast good faith and indomitable resolution of the British. It is as if one were gazing into a kaleidoscope—anon the terra cotta hue of the Bráhmin suffuses the vision—anon it is blurred out by the saffron shade of the true Mahratta—that again is obliterated by the rose-pink of Central India, while Hôlkar dominates—this deepens into the lurid red of Sindia's times, which is again washed out in rose-colour—that gives place again to the Bráhmin brick-dust shade, clouded over and over again by dark shadows of deceit and treachery—

the while, as the hand turns, in each picture appear fragments of the Môgul green—until at last all tints blend in bewildering confusion, and the "red, white and blue" of the English nation effacing them all, remains permanently reflected by the prismatic glasses.

In 1797 Náná Furnáwees re-organised his ministry, which had first to deal with a desperate affray between the Arabs of the Môguls and a party of the Peishwa's regulars under the Major Boyd: when one hundred were killed on the spot and the bazars were generally looted. On the 15th August Tookajee Hôlkar died, and at once dissensions arose between his two legitimate and two illegitimate sons as to the succession. Khâssee Rao, the elder of the former, was an imbecile, yet Sindia supported him: but Náná Furnáwees secretly favoured the younger Mulhár Rao, until he was attacked and killed by Sindia in the outskirts of Poona, and his two half-brothers, Jèswant Rao and Wittojee, fled the city. Thus did the house of Hôlkar for a time become subservient to the house of Sindia; thus did the power of Náná Furnáwees receive its death-blow, for Sindia began to interfere in all affairs of state, and Bájee Rao, with fatuous treachery, egged him on through the infamous Ghàtgay Shirzee Rao, whom he persuaded that Náná's influence alone stood in the way of his becoming Sindia's prime minister.

Accordingly on the 31st December, Ghátgay caused the old minister, though his personal safety had been guaranteed by Sindia himself, to be seized at a visit of ceremony, with several of his followers. Their palaces were besieged, some were plundered, and "The City of Poona was like a town taken by storm; the firing continued the whole of the night and the ensuing day". Bàjee Rao simultaneously did his part by arresting all Náná's ministers in open durbar. Náná was imprisoned at Ahmednuggur; and Bájee Rao having thus, as he fancied, got rid of his aged friend, set to work to rid himself of Sindia also. But first of all it was necessary to satisfy some of Sindia's soldiery; to do this Bájee Rao actually consented, if he did not incite, Ghátgay and his ruffians to levy a contribution from the merchants, bankers and all persons supposed to possess wealth in the city. The Ex-Ministers were dragged forth, maltreated, scourged and tortured so that several of them died, and the streets were strewn with dead and wounded. Bájee Rao then fomented discord in Sindia's army, and when he thought it was ripe for revolt, ordered Dowlut Rao Sindia to wait upon him, when it had been arranged that Sindia should be seized. But Bájee's Rao courage, as usual, failed him at the critical moment; Sindia got away to his camp, and continued to oppress Poona, while Bájee Rao raised a rebellion at Sátára, which if it had not been quelled by Sindia would have effectually wiped out the Bráhmins.

Then arose the domestic dissensions known as "the revolt of the Byes or three widows of Mhádáji Rao Sindia, and the Shènwee Bráhmin Ministers." Of this, as the principal incidents did not occur in Poona, it is sufficient to say that the immediate result was that Khássee Rao Hôlkar espoused the cause of the Byes, while Bájee Rao allied himself with

Nizám Ally "through his resident envoys, then at Poona."

Sindia, now alarmed, became very desirous of obtaining that mediation which he had before refused from the British Government. Col. Palmer, the British Agent, advised him to restore his Shènwee Ministry, to settle amicably with the Byes, and to submit formally to the authority of the Peishwa; but Sindia saw, or thought he saw a better way, in the release of Náná Furnáwees, which he promptly followed by the revocation of the treaty with Nizám Ally. Thereupon Bájee Rao played his trump card by entering into negotiations with both Náná and Sindia, who at last, seriously alarmed at his unpopularity by reason of Ghátgay Shirzee Rao's cruel excesses, caused that arch-fiend to be captured, and removed, to the intense relief of Poona City. Sindia and Bájee Rao then became reconciled with the full approval of the British Government, which under Lord Mornington, temporarily abandoned the policy of neutrality in preparation for its great struggle with Tippoo Sahèb and his French Allies (1798).

## CHAPTER III.

### Historical Sketch—*Continued.* (1800 to 1816).

Death of Náná Furnáwees—Hôlkar and Sindia—The Battle of Poona--Flight of Bájee Rao—Treaty of Bassein no sooner signed than Bájee Rao intrigues against it—Trimbuckjee Dainglià—Humiliation of Bájee Rao.

THE year 1800 was momentous for the City of Poona. On the 13th March Náná Furnáwees died "and with him," truly said Colonel Palmer the British Resident, "departed all the wisdom and moderation of the Mahratta Government." Despite his personal cowardice and his unprincipled ambition, he always displayed great moral courage and a tenacity of purpose which gained for him extraordinary influence over his countrymen, so that at times, and there were many, when his career seemed terminated by the machinations of his secret enemies, he rose to the occasion, and defeated them all. In private, if not in public life, he was strictly truthful, humane, frugal and charitable. "He was a patriot, if ever there was a Bráhmin patriot." No matter what the consequences might be to himself personally, he always advised Bájee Rao to be moderate and circumspect. His sagacity told him that the only really dangerous foe of the Mahratta Empire was the British Government, which he highly respected for its honesty and vigour, but he feared it, for its patience, pertinacity, and indomitable resolution. He never attributed, as most Asiatics are prone to do, its forbearance and moderation to fear. He alone perhaps among all Asiatic statesmen of the time, knew and thoroughly appreciated the English character, and he foresaw that with the rise of English power must decline, not merely Brahminical influence, but the ascendency of his nation. "Náná Furnawees was certainly a great statesman."

He was scarcely cremated when Bájee Rao and Sindia began to quarrel about the vast riches he was believed to have amassed. Sindia promptly seized the dead minister's "jágheer", and urged his widow to adopt a son as the easiest means of securing the treasure and annoying Bájee Rao. Bájee Rao, on the other hand, worked through spies and secret agents and retaliated by inducing Sindia to destroy his recently reinstated Shenwee Ministers. Bálloba Táttya was thereupon imprisoned at Ahmednuggur, where, fortunately for himself, he died before he could be tortured, but his brother Dhôndeba and the Bakshee (or Commander-in-Chief) were barbarously executed at Poona, the former being blown from a gun, the latter "by being tied round with rockets, which being fired, carried him along, mangling his body dreadfully." As a matter of fact Náná Furnáwees's reputed treasures have never been traced to the present day.

The next act of the vindictive Bájee Rao was to destroy Náná's friends, among them the family of Purèshram Bhow, who had been his own great supporter at most critical times. That did not matter to this incarnate fiend—Purèshram Bhow had been the friend of Nánà, *ergo* his family and their friends must be punished; so he invited them all to his palace at Poona to discuss the question of the widow adopting a son, there seized them and sent them off to various hill forts.

Towards the end of 1800 Sindia became alarmed at the successes of Jèswant Rao Hôlkar in Málwa, and left Poona to encounter him: Khâssee Rao Hôlkar, it will be remembered, was still in Poona. Here was an opportunity for Bájee Rao to conciliate all parties and thus to re-establish his authority as Peishwa, with the moral and material support of the British Government. But Bájee Rao, left to himself, was incapable of rising to any emergency: his malignant mind was bent only on revenge—he continued to hunt down every high Bráhmin family that had even excited his ill-will, the Patwardhans, the Rástias, and the Poorundharees. Thus "the minds of his subjects were alienated, distrust and disaffection toward Bájee Rao's power and government became almost universal," and anarchy spread throughout the country. Wittoojee Hôlkar, marauding on his brother's account in the vicinity of Poona, was taken prisoner and brought before Bájee Rao, who could not forget that his father Tookajee had been the friend of Nánà Furnáwees. Before the palace, Wittoojee, beseeching mercy, was tied to the foot of an elephant and dragged about the yard and into the streets, Bájee Rao the while seated in a balcony drinking in his screams.

Sindia of course was delighted at this removal of one of the Hôlkar brothers, but Jèswant Rao Hôlkar vowed vengeance—whereupon the cowardly Bájee Rao actually opened negotiations with him, promised to recognise him as the head of the house of Hôlkar, and inveighing against the Shirzee Rao Ghátgay (Sindia's infamous father-in-law before mentioned), tried, but failed, to seize him. Escaping by an act of marvellous daring, Ghátgay encamped outside Poona, which he threatened to sack and burn. Meantime Bájee Rao invoked the mediation of the British Resident with the incensed Sindia, and the latter being sorely in need of his boldest commander, called Ghátgay off to Málwa. The City of Poona was thus at last rid of the fiend who for years had terrorised over everyone, plundered, tortured, and murdered in it, at his own sweet will.

Pushing on to Indore (Hôlkar's capital), Ghátgay signally defeated Jèswant Rao Hôlkar (October 14th, 1801), but Sindia did not follow up the blow. Jèswant Rao Hôlkar had time to rally his forces, and within a year an immense force appeared at Poona. Bájee Rao at once sought British aid, but he was so obviously insincere, that it was refused. He then fawned upon Jèswant Rao. "My brother Wittoojee," replied Jèswant Rao, "is dead, he cannot be restored to me; but let my nephew Khundee Rao be released, and the family possessions given up." Bájee Rao, to gain time, while he urged Sindia to push on to Poona with all speed, pretended to assent, but really hurried Khundee Rao off to prison in Asseergurh. Sindia and Hôlkar then each raced for Poona, where Jèswant Rao Hôlkar arrived first, on the 23rd October, 1802, encamping a few miles off at Lônee—Sindia arrived next day, and encamped between the British Camp at Kirkee and the City.

On the morning of the 25th October, the two great Mahratta Armies confronted each other in battle array. History does not record a stranger scene. On one side lay the City of Poona wherein sat the Bráhmin Peishwa, his motley force of Arabs, Môguls, Pathans, half-drilled Mahratta Infantry and mobs of irregular horsemen ready to take part in the battle directly it should turn in Sindia's favour. On the other side drawn up under arms in their cantonment at Kirkee, the handful of well-disciplined British troops under Colonel Close, who—just as "off side" is marked off at the Rugby game of football—had set up the British standard at prominent points round the Residency (at the Sungum) and the Camp. The British Army was not to intervene under any circumstances, but simply to protect its position from both combatants.

There were English officers commanding in each Mahratta army.

Jèswant Rao Hôlkar had 14 regiments of regular infantry, divided into three brigades, commanded respectively by Colonel Vickers, Major Harding, and Major Armstrong; five thousand irregular infantry, twenty-five thousand cavalry, and more than 100 guns, were distributed among the three brigades.

Sindia's army was commanded by Sewdáseo Bhow

Bhâskur with Captain Dawes his chief of the Staff as it were. Under him were ten regular regiments of infantry —six of them without European officers—four, the old battalions of De Boigne, led by Frenchmen and Neapolitans. Sewdáseo Bhow's irregular infantry, cavalry and artillery were more numerous than Hôlkar's, without the Peishwa's force held in reserve in the City.

The ball opened by a tremendous but not very deadly cannonade for two and a half hours. Then Hôlkar launched his Pathan Cavalry at the horse of the Chief of Vinchoor and dispersed them, but his Mahratta cavalry were at the same time repulsed with heavy loss in a similar attack on the Peishwa's "Hoojrât Págah" or body-guard. Sewdáseo Bhow followed up this success so vigorously that the defeat of his opponent seemed imminent, when Jèswant Rao Hôlkar himself sprang on his horse, shouting "Now or never follow Jèswant Rao," rallied the fugitives, turned on Sindia's horse, and drove them back.

Meanwhile, Colonel Vickers was defeating Sindia's six regiments without European officers, and Harding and Armstrong were being stoutly resisted by De Boigne's old battalions. At this critical moment, Jèswant Rao, having just driven off Sindia's cavalry, fell upon them and the supporting artillery, killed three out of the four European officers, took the fourth prisoner, and cut down the gunners at their gnns. A general rout of Sindia's army followed and all his guns and baggage fell into Hôlkar's hands. Thus ended this remarkable engagement, which resulted in the final withdrawal of Sindia from the vicinity of Poona.

Bájee Rao had felt confident of Sindia's success, and was ready to fall on Hôlkar with his reserves when the tide turned in the former's favour, but "the firing frightened him," and he proceeded to the south or safe side of the City, whence he bolted to Singurh directly the rout began. From Singurh he hastily appealed to Colonel Close for protection, forwarding a preliminary treaty by which he engaged "to subsidise six battalions of Sepoys, and to cede 25 lakhs of rupees of annual revenue for their support." The British Resident, however, preserved his attitude of strict neutrality. Bájee Rao then fled from Singurh to Raigurh, from Raigurh to Mhar, whence he besought the British Government to take him by sea. Hotly pursued by Hôlkar's troops, he fled again to Severndroog (Hurnee) Fort, but again alarmed took ship to Rewadunda, where a British ship put in and took him to Bassein, where for the moment I will leave the coward, to return to the victorious Hôlkar.

On the morning after his great victory Colonel Close, "on the urgent invitation of Hôlkar, visited him in his camp. He found the conqueror in a small tent, ankle-deep in mud, wounded by a spear, and with a sabre cut in the head, which he had received from an artillery man in one of the charges." He was in high spirits, laughed at his wounds, and was particularly cordial to the British Agent, whom he begged to mediate with Sindia and the Peishwa, but Colonel Close had not yet received instructions to depart from the policy of neutrality.

Jèswant Rao, true to the humane traditions of his house in its dealings with the City, placed out-posts around to prevent plundering, was kind and humane to the Peishwa's dependants and sent Bájee Rao many messages to return to Poona.

The Hôlkars were always distinguished for comparative moderation in their behaviour toward the defenceless city, and even then, though flushed with victory and compelled by impecuniosity to obtain money to pay his troops, Jèswant Rao made his levies on the citizens with some regard to fairness and decorum. He also made many improvements in the approaches to the city, among them the wooden bridge over the Moolla at Kirkee, which, still standing, is known as "Hôlkar's bridge". From the Sindias and their myrmidons, on the contrary, the people of Poona never received other than barbarous and cruel treatment. Yet Sindia would even now be received with acclamation in the city, while a visit from Hôlkar would be regarded with indifference!

When Jèswant Rao Hôlkar found that Bájee Rao would not return to Poona, he bethought himself of the latter's second brother, Amrut Rao, then at Joonere, sent for him, and with some difficulty persuaded him to assume government, aided by certain old ministers of Náná Furnáwees. At first Amrut Rao refused to ascend his brother's throne or to let his own son be nominated, but when Bájee Rao fled from Mhár and sought British protection he regarded this as abdication. The Rájá of Sátára was not easily induced to give his consent, but at last Amrut Rao was installed as Peishwa (end of November, 1802). The first thing he did was to egg on Hôlkar to plunder Poona, just as his brother Bájee Rao had previously egged on Sindia to rapine through Ghâtgay Shirzee Rao.

The outrages, tortures and murders of the Shirzee Rao were even surpassed, and poor Poona never had a worse time, especially as all exits from the city were closely guarded. The British Resident was detained by the usurpers in the hope that he would mediate with Sindia, and induce the Bombay Government to recognise the usurpation, but Colonel Close left Poona in disgust on the 20th November, and arriving at Bombay on 3rd December, met Bájee Rao when he was landed at Bassein from Rewadunda, and on the last day of the year concluded with him the celebrated Treaty of Bassein which regulated the relations of the Court of Poona and the British Government until the final downfall of the Peishwa in 1817.

Bájee Rao, as a matter of course, had no sooner signed than he sought to stultify the Treaty, to conciliate Sindia and Rughoojee Bhonslay, who he knew would not approve of the British alliance. Sindia was asked to proceed to Poona "to punish the rebel Hôlkar," but Sindia had had enough of that game, and set himself with Bhonslay to organise "a general confederacy of the Mahrattas against the common enemy" the British Government, Bájee Rao secretly aiding and abetting the scheme.

Ignorant of the conspiracy, the Governor-General began to take measures to reinstate Bájee Rao in accordance with the Treaty. More than 20,000 troops were sent from Hyderabad to the Mahratta frontier, and General Wellesley (afterwards Duke of Wellington), the Commander-in-Chief at Madras, hurried up to the Krishna, where he was joined by all the Southern Sirdars, and proceeded to Poona, which he reached on the 20th April, 1803, after a forced march of 60 miles in 32 hours, fearing that Amrut Rao and Hôlkar would burn the city. The usurpers, however, had already made themselves scarce, Jèswant Rao Hôlkar plundering his way along the Nizám's frontier towards Málwá, while Amrut Rao turned north-west, looting all towns and villages till he reached Nassick "which he pillaged in the same barbarous manner as he had Poona." This worthy, never reconciled to his brother Bájee Rao, ultimately joined the British armies, with a body of horse, with which he did no great service, but was nevertheless granted the absurdly extravagant pension of eight lakhs of rupees, with which he retired to Benares.

On the 13th May Bájee Rao, escorted by some 2,500 British troops, was reseated on the "musnud."

Meantime the Governor-General, apprised of the Mahratta Confederacy, strove to detach Hôlkar from it, but succeeded only in so far that the latter retreated to Málwá to sit neutral till he saw a fitting moment to chime in. It remained for the Governor-General to attack the other confederates simultaneously from all sides of India. Then followed that splendid series of victories by General Wellesley at Ahmednuggur, Assaye, and Asseergurh, and by Lake at Aligurh, Delhi, Agra, Láswarree and Gowelgurh. With these, or with the treaties with the Rájpoot chiefs, or the temporary successes of Hôlkar against Monson in the north-west, the city of Poona was only concerned in so far as the general result was necessarily to establish British power more firmly in the Deccan, till the time came when (1809) Jèswant Rao Hôlkar having become insane, the Shirzee Rao Ghâtgay (1809) being at last killed by Sindia's orders, and the British Government having generously interposed to clear Rughoojee Bhonslay's territories of the freebooters (called Pindarrees), a brief lull ensued in which some settlement seemed practicable. But the Pindarrees soon gathered in greater numbers, and practically overran all Central India till they were finally extirpated in 1816 by British armies, never having ventured nearer Poona than the Berárs.

We left Bájee Rao (1803) re-established at Poona as Peishwa by British arms and influence, but already casting about in his mind how he might secretly, if not openly, nullify the Treaty of Bassein with the Power that had befriended him.

Grant Duff suggests that he was actuated by motives of revenge, but he had no wrongs from the English to avenge. He can only have been prompted, snakelike, by sheer malignity to bite the bosom that cherished him. He maintained up to the last moment secret relations with Sindia, Hôlkar and Rughoojee Bhônslay, and instructed his agent at Hyderabad to involve the Nizám in the confederacy against the English at the moment they were engaged in the last war with Tippoo Sahèb: his machinations might have been successful there if Seringapatam had not speedily fallen and Tippoo been killed. Thus employing, as it were, his leisure moments, he renewed his persecutions of his friends among the Deccan Sirdars; the Rastia family which had served him so well and even now was doing him good service in an insurrection of his troops, was disgraced without reason: the Pritineedhee was driven into rebellion, severely wounded, captured and imprisoned in the City of Poona, his jagheer mostly confiscated, his private property and all his family jewellery appropriated and never accounted for by the Peishwa's agent (Bappoo Gôhlà): the persecution of the Putwardhaus was renewed, and no friend or descendant of a friend or adherent of Náná Furnáwees was left unmolested; "whilst thus engaged, Bájee Rao was happy."

All this time nothing could be sweeter or more seemingly grateful than Bájee Rao's behaviour to the British Resident. He was, he said, fondly attached to Colonel Close personally; he never did anything—not he—without consulting him; he blessed the British Government for all the benefits it had showered on him, for its hospitality when a fugitive, for its countenance, moral and physical support, and for its restoration of him to the "musnud." To some extent he may have imposed on Colonel Close, but it was otherwise with Mr. Mountstuart Elphinstone who succeeded to the Residentship in 1810. Mr. Elphinstone had been Colonel Close's assistant at the end of the preceding century; he had been attached to General Wellesley's staff in 1803; he was one of the old "*Chár durwaza koola*" (the four-doors-open School), who saw and communicated with all natives himself. A man of high culture and great literary ability, he knew the languages well, had studied the histories of all the great families, was versed in native character and especially knew his Bráhmin down to the ground: Bájee Rao never deceived him for a moment; with marvellous sagacity he saw through all his schemes, with incredible patience he tracked or anticipated his intrigues and quietly frustrated them. He was ably seconded by his friend and Assistant, Capt. Grant Duff, the historian, who had Mahratta history at his finger's ends.

It was easy for such a master-mind afterwards to see through Bájee Rao's attempts to corrupt his Parsee confidential Agent, Khoosroji Moodhee (of whom more anon), and to perceive the Peishwa's object in appointing him to the Government of a Mahratta Province; but Mr. Elphinstone was powerless, when the Parsee's downfall came, to prevent the nomination of the infamous Trimbuckjee Dainglià as his successor. This man, originally a spy or messenger, who had ingratiated himself with Bájee Rao when he fled to Mhár (in 1802), by carrying a letter to Poona and bringing back an answer in an incredibly short time, was attached to the Peishwa's person. Possessed of extraordinary energy and intelligence, and absolutely unscrupulous, Trimbuckjee pandered to his vices and, as he once told Mr. Elphinstone, "if his master ordered him he would kill a cow,"—about as strong an impious declaration of servility as a Mahratta could make! From the Government of the Carnatic Trimbuckjee soon rose to be the Peishwa's representative minister at the British Residency; murder, torture, and abduction were his pastimes, and Bájee Rao connived at all. So great became his influence that he got himself made "Sur-Soobbedar" (or Governor-General) of the Peishwa's districts in Guzerat; this brought him into collision with the important minister, Gungádhur Shâstree, who, imprudently venturing to Poona, was decoyed to Punderpoor and there treacherously murdered by Trimbuckjee, undoubtedly under Bájee Rao's instructions. This was more than the British Resident could bear, and he compelled Bájee Rao to deliver up his favourite Trimbuckjee, who was then imprisoned in the British Gaol Fort at Tannah; but on the 12th Sept., 1816, the monster cleverly escaped, took to the Syádree Hills between Poona and Nassik, raised the Rámoosees, Bheels and Mángs, with money lavishly supplied by Bájee Rao, and began to plunder the country-side.

Called to account for this rebellion by Mr. Elphinstone, Bájee Rao at first actually denied that it existed, insisting that the offenders were Pindarree free-booters from Central India. Forced at last to despatch troops to the neighbourhood, he sent in false reports that the robbers had been attacked and dispersed; but the Resident was not to be fooled, and at last Bájee Rao could no longer deny the insurrection. He was given every opportunity of repentance, and of himself actively suppressing it, but he failed, and British troops had to take the field. Just at this time Mr. Elphinstone received a private letter from Calcutta, which mentioned that Trimbuckjee, Dainglià's surrender must be the first step to any further negotiations. A conference was arranged, whereat Bájee Rao exerted all his eloquence in vain; Mr. Elphinstone stood firm, gave Bájee Rao one month to surrender Trimbuckjee, and insisted on the immediate delivery to British custody of the three Forts of Singurh, Raigurh and Poorundhur. Bájee Rao still temporised, unable to believe that the Resident would fulfil his threats, hoping to gain time for the Mahratta confederacy to open hostilities. Mr. Elphinstone, however, was not to be denied. On the 7th May he informed Bájee Rao that he was about to surround the City of Poona. Bájee Rao still held back, and Mr. Elphinstone promptly carried out his threat, whereupon, Bájee Rao at last caved in, sent out his orders to the Killadars (Fort Governors) to give up the Forts, and proclaimed a reward of two lakhs of rupees and a village in "enam" of Rs. 1000 for the apprehension of Trimbuckjee Dainglià alive or dead.

On the 10th of May the Governor-General's instructions reached Mr. Elphinstone. In pursuance of them a new Treaty was executed in which Bájee Rao had (first) to admit that Trimbuckjee Dainglià had murdered Gungádhur Shâstree while "residing under the guarantee of the British Government within the Peishwa's territory": (secondly) to give up Trimbuckjee's family as hostages till the monster himself should be arrested: (thirdly) to bind himself to hold no communication with any foreign power, and, "as head of the Mahratta Empire", to renounce all dominions beyond the Nerbuddah and Toongbuddra rivers: (fourthly) to settle with the Gaekwár as stipulated: (fifthly) to cede territory yielding 34 lakhs to pay for a contingent of 5,000 Horse and 3,000 Infantry: (sixthly) to cede the Fort of Ahmednuggur and all his rights to territory north of the Nerbuddah: (seventhly) to observe the settlement of 1812 with his Jagheerdars, which meant restitution to most of them, including the much wronged Rástia family: (eighthly) to vacate certain places on the Môgulai or Nizám's frontier, which his troops had wrongfully occupied since 1811.

The humiliation of Bájee Rao was complete, and it was confidently believed that he *would* observe *this* Treaty. He began by reducing his cavalry, but it was afterwards discovered that their disbandment was only nominal. What he really did was to grant the Silladars (Commandants) seven months' leave on full pay *in advance*, with strict injunctions to remain at home and be ready to join him with all troopers at a moment's notice! Bájee Rao, availed himself of the earliest opportunity of interviewing Sir John Malcolm, then holding the high office of Political Agent of the Governor-General. The conference took place at Máholee, near Sátára, when Sir John Malcolm—"douce mon"—was so completely taken in by his protestations of gratitude, his promises of amendment and his lamentations, that he went to Poona and urged Mr. Elphinstone to treat the poor Peishwa with confidence, and to let him increase rather than disband his troops! Mr. Elphinstone smiled grimly as he promised "to keep kind" on Bájee Rao, but he pointed out that his game was to take advantage of the main British Force under Colonel Smith being at a distance, while only a handful of British troops remained at Poona. Mr. Elphinstone further warned Sir John what would certainly happen in a few weeks. His predictions were literally fulfilled—how, I will relate as far as possible in Captain Grant Duff's own words.

## CHAPTER IV.

### Historical Sketch—*Completed.* (1817—1818.)

The Downfall of the Peishwa.—The Battle of Kirkee.— British annexation.—The Infamy of Bájee Rao.

THE forts of Singurh, Raigurh, and Poorundhur were restored to the Peishwa during the month of August. The excessively heavy rains of this season, prolonged to an unusually late date, delayed the advance of the whole Deccan (British) army. Brigadier-General Smith had transported his division across the Ghauts by the 9th October, and by the 20th occupied convenient positions close to the Chándore range of hills, with a view of advancing into Khándeish, as soon as it should appear requisite. A battalion of light infantry, with some auxiliary horse, were left between Seroor and Ahmednuggur; one auxiliary battalion was stationed for the protection of the Seroor cantonment, and the Peishwa's own corps, consisting of from 400 to 500 men, remained at Dâpooree in its first cantonment, a few miles to the north-west of Poona. The Company's European regiment from Bombay was to be held in readiness to join the brigade at Poona about the end of October.

The Peishwa did not return to his capital until the end

of September. During his stay at Mâholy he was most actively engaged in the schemes he had long meditated against the British Government; but, by the advice of Bappoo Gôklá, he had determined on changing his plans of covert hostility to an open attack, as soon as he should be prepared.

The recommendation of Sir John Malcolm to recruit his army, for the purpose of aiding in the Pindárree war, afforded an excellent cloak to his designs. Gôklá was now the leader of all his measures, and Bájee Rao was induced to give him a formal writing under his own seal, which he confirmed on oath, binding himself to be implicitly directed by his counsel, and investing him with the full powers of his government. This measure seems to have been adopted not merely as a security to Gôklá, but as a means of allaying the mistrust which the commandant sillidars entertained towards Bájee Rao, and was the condition on which several of the Jágheerdars and chiefs pledged themselves to stand by him. This circumstance, though reported in the country, was not fully ascertained until after the commencement of hostilities. Bappoo Gôklá received ten millions of rupees—nearly a million sterling—to assist in the expense of preparation. From the time of his first determination to break with the English, Bájee Rao had restored the lands of many of his jágheerdars, and for several years had been endeavouring to render himself more popular with all classes of his subjects. He unfolded his intention of going to war with the English to the Rájá of Sátára, and, while he exacted from him and his mother an oath of secrecy and support, he sent them and all their family into strict confinement in Wâssóta. His recruiting went forward with remarkable activity, his forts also were garrisoned, stored, and repaired; and orders issued to prepare his fleet.

Many Bheels and Rámoosees were engaged in his interest by Trimbuckjee Daingliá; and special missions were despatched to Nâgpoor and the camps of Sindia, Hôlkar, and Umeer Khan, the Pindarree leader; the schemes which Bájee Rao personally directed were the seduction of the native troops and the assassination of the Resident. His plan of corrupting the troops extended even to the European officers; and the agent employed for the latter purpose was one Jèswunt Rao Ghorepuray, who for many years had resided at Poona, was intimately acquainted with many of the officers, and received a pension from the British Government.

Bájee Rao, judging the opportunity favourable, sent for Jéswunt Rao, and, after many promises, exacting an oath of secrecy, communicated the plan for corrupting the European officers—a commission which Jèswunt Rao, although he well knew its futility, like a true Mahratta, readily undertook, upon receiving an advance of 50,000 rupees. So far he kept his oath as to say nothing of these circumstances; but Jèswunt Rao had a great personal regard for Mr. Elphinstone, and, throughout the rise and progress of the Peishwa's preparations, gave early and constant warning of what might be expected.

The reports of corrupting the troops were brought from all quarters; some of the sepoys indignantly refused what, to them, were splendid offers, and others, pretending to acquiesce, communicated the circumstances to their officers. But the extent of the intrigues could not be ascertained, and they at last became alarming even to those who knew the fidelity of the Bombay sepoys, from the circumstance of the Peishwa having many of their families and relations in his power, against whom he commenced a system of persecution, which he threatened to perpetuate if the sepoys refused to desert the British service.

It was the Peishwa's wish, previous to the commencement of hostilities, to invite Mr. Elphinstone to a conference, and murder him; but this plan was opposed by Gôklá, who, though he concurred in the plan of corrupting the sepoys, and was most sanguine in his belief of complete success, disdained to perpetrate so base a crime, especially as Mr. Elphinstone had more than once proved himself his friend. But Bájee Rao was unwilling to relinquish a favourite scheme of personal revenge, and proposed to assassinate the Resident as he rode out; or, should that fail, to get Trimbuckjee, with a body of Bheels, to endeavour to surprise the Residency by night, whilst a simultaneous attack should be made on the cantonment.

The last interview that took place between Mr. Elphinstone and the Peishwa was on the 14th of October, when, although the latter adverted to the loss of territory and reputation he had suffered by the late treaty, he continued to express grateful ackowledgments for the former friendship of the British Government. On Mr. Elphinstone's mentioning how anxiously the advance of the troops was desired, Bájee Rao repeated the assurances which he had of late frequently made through his ministers, that *his* own troops should be sent to the frontier to co-operate against the Pindarrees immediately after the Dussera.

The festival of the Dussera took place on the 10th October, and was the most splendid military spectacle ever witnessed since the accession of Bájee Rao. Two circumstances were particularly observable on this occasion; 1st, a marked degree of slight towards the British Resident; 2nd, at the moment of the Peishwa's quitting the ground, a large mass of horse, under one Nároo Punt Aptey, galloped down, as if to charge the flank of the British troops, but wheeled round as they came near. The intention of this manœuvre was to show the British sepoys their insignificance when compared to this host of Mahratta spears. It was supposed it would have effect in aiding the Peishwa's intrigues. It would have been difficult to convince the Mahrattas, in that vaunting moment, that of the three weak battalions then peaceably and unsuspectingly standing before them, one, in less than three months, would repulse their whole army!

After the Dussera every day became more interesting, and by the 25th parties of the Peishwa's troops were coming into Poona from all quarters, by day and night. General Smith's force was still at a distance, and the European regiment from Bombay could hardly be expected in less than ten days. The position occupied by the British brigade almost joined the northern environs of Poona; it had been originally taken up by Sir Arthur Wellesley for the protection of the city, but circumstances were now reversed. Gardens and enclosures with prickly-pear hedges ran in many places within half-musket-shot of the lines, affording not only every advantage for the attack of the Arabs and irregulars, but, in case of disaffection amongst the sepoys, every facility to desert. Small parties of horse came out of the city and encamped round the British cantonment; in a few days they augmented to large bodies, whilst a strong corps of Gósâveen infantry occupied a position on one of the flanks.

The Sungum being at some distance from the cantonment, the Vinchoorkur's horse, with some infantry and guns, coolly encamped between the Residency and the village of Bámbooree; but besides these preparations, all reports concurred in representing that an immediate attack was meditated.

For several nights the Peishwa and his advisers had deliberated on the advantage of surprising the troops before the arrival of the European regiment; and for this purpose, on the 28th October, their guns were yoked, their horses saddled, and their infantry in readiness. This intelligence was brought to Mr. Elphinstone a little before midnight of the 28th, and for a moment it became a question whether self-defence did not require that the attack should be anticipated.

It was an hour of anxiety: the British cantonment and the Residency were perfectly still, and the inhabitants slept in complete repose, inspired by confidence, in that profound peace to which they had been long accustomed; but in the Peishwa's camp, south of the town, all was noise and uproar. Mr. Elphinstone had as yet betrayed no suspicion of the Peishwa's treachery, and, as he now stood listening on the terrace, he probably thought that in thus exposing his troops to be cut off without even the satisfaction of dying with arms in their hands, he had followed the system of confidence, so strongly recommended, to a culpable extremity. But other motives influenced his conduct at this important moment. He was aware how little faith the Mahratta princes placed in Bájee Rao, and that Sindia, who knew him well, would hesitate to engage in hostilities until the Peishwa had fairly committed himself. Apprised of the Governor-General's secret plans, and his intended movements on Gwalior—which many circumstances might have concurred to postpone—Mr. Elphinstone had studiously avoided every appearance that might affect the negotiations in Hindostan, and any preparation that might give Sindia's secret emissaries at Poona reason to believe that war was inevitable. To have sent to the cantonment at that hour would have occasioned considerable stir; and in the meantime, by the reports of the spies, the Peishwa was evidently deliberating; the din in the city was dying away; the night was passing, and the motives which had hitherto prevented preparation, determined Mr. Elphinstone to defer it some hours longer. Major J. A. Wilson, the officer in command of the European regiment on its march from Bombay, had already been made acquainted with the critical state of affairs, and was hastening forward.

Next morning, however, the officer in command of the brigade at Poona was requested to keep the men ready in their lines, but with as little appearance of bustle as possible. At three o'clock in the afternoon, Mr. Elphinstone sent a message to the Peishwa, mentioning that his Highness's horsemen were crowding in upon the position of the brigade, that such a mode of encamping had never been practised or permitted by British troops, and therefore the commanding officer confined his men to their cantonment until those of his Highness should be withdrawn, lest, by their contiguity, disputes might arise between them. This message was delivered by Captain Ford, and created a great sensation.

Gôklà recommended that the attack should not be delayed, but the Peishwa hesitated, stating that he wished a little more time to make sure of corrupting the sepoys; the European regiment was still, as he believed, at a great distance, and every hour was adding to his own army. Another night was thus wasted in consultation, and at four o'clock of the following afternoon (30th October) the European regiment by great exertions marched into the cantonment. Mr. Elphinstone now determined on removing the troops from their unsafe position to another in many respects more eligible, at the village of Kirkee, four miles distant, which had been early pointed out by General Smith as the proper one to be occupied in case of an apprehended rupture. The troops accordingly took up their ground at Kirkee on the 1st November, and the Residency being close to the town, 250 men were sent for its protection. The Peishwa was apprised of the intended movement; but his army supposed that the British troops had withdrawn from fear, and was much encouraged in consequence.

The vacated cantonment was plundered; an officer, on his route to Bombay was attacked, wounded, and robbed in open day; the language of the Peishwa's ministers was most slighting; his troops everywhere began to insult passers-by, while they continued defiantly to push forward. They began to form a camp betwixt the old cantonment and the new position, and a party of their horse moved down to the spot. A second message was therefore sent to the Peishwa, begging that the motives of the British movement might not be misconstrued; for if the British troops were pressed upon as in the old position, those of his Highness must be treated as enemies. The Peishwa now believed, from the reports of his emissaries, that the British sepoys were completely seduced. On the 4th November, Móró Dixit, a minister who had formed an attachment to Major Ford, and was anxious to save him, communicated this intelligence, adding that his master was determined to cut off the British detachment without sparing a man.

On the 3rd November Mr. Elphinstone directed the light battalion and a party of auxiliary horse stationed at Seroor, to move to Poona. As soon as the news of these arrangements reached the Peishwa, he determined to delay the attack no longer. His preparations began about seven o'clock on the morning of the 5th; but in the early part of the day he sent out several messages calculated to lull the Resident's suspicions; such as, "his troops were alarmed by hearing that those at Kirkee were under arms";—"he was about to perform a religious ceremony at the temple of Párbuttee, and the troops were drawn out, in honour of the occasion, to form a street as he passed." In the afternoon, when all was in readiness, his principal officers having assembled at his palace, Wittoojee Gaekwár, a personal servant of the Peishwa, was despatched to Mr. Elphinstone, by Gôklà's advice, to inform him that the assembly of troops at Poona was very offensive to the Peishwa; to desire him to send away the European regiment—to reduce the native brigade to its usual strength, when it must occupy a position which the Peishwa would point out, and that if these demands were not complied with he (the Resident) could withdraw from Poona and never return! Mr. Elphinstone denied the Peishwa's right to require the removal of the European regiment, explained the reason of his having called in the light battalion, and recommended that the Peishwa should send his troops to the frontier as he had promised, in which case all cause of complaint would be removed. Much more passed, as the conversation on the part of the messenger was intended to engage as much attention as possible; but he at last withdrew, warning the Resident of the bad consequences of his refusal. In the meantime the Peishwa's officers at the palace were despatched to their troops; Bájee Rao in person proceeded to the Párbuttee Temple and Palace; and Wittoojee Gaekwár had scarcely quitted the Residency when intelligence was brought that the Peishwa's army was moving out on the west side of the city.

There was a momentary consultation about defending the Residency, but it was instantly abandoned as impracticable, and it was determined to retire to Kirkee, for which purpose the nature of the ground afforded great facility. The river Moola betwixt the Sungum and the village of Kirkee forms two curves like the letter S inverted. The Residency and the village were both on the same side of the river, but at the former there was a ford, and near the latter a bridge (Hôlkar's); so that a party, by crossing at the ford, had the river between them and the Peishwa's troops the greater part of the way. From the Residency no part of the Mahratta army was visible excepting bodies of infantry, which were assembled along the tops of the adjoining heights, with the intention of cutting off the Residency from the camp, and having this object in view, they did not molest individuals. On ascending one of the eminences on which they were forming, the plain beneath must have presented at that moment a most imposing spectacle. This plain, then covered with grain, terminates on the west by a range of small hills, while on the east it is bounded by the city of Poona and the small hills already partially occupied by the infantry. A mass of cavalry covered nearly the whole extent of it, and towards the city endless streams of horsemen were pouring from every avenue.

Mr. Elphinstone had personally reconnoitred the ground in front of the village of Kirkee, and ascertained that there was a ford between that village and Dápooree, which, although difficult, was practicable for six-pounders, three of which, manned by native artillerymen, belonged to the auxiliary force and was attached to Captain Ford's corps. It had been arranged, in case of an attack, that Captain Ford was to join the brigade under Lieutenant-Colonel Burr; and Mr. Elphinstone had been at pains to explain to all concerned the advantage of always acting on the offensive against Mahrattas. When the party was fording at the Residency, a messenger was despatched to warn the troops of the approach of the enemy. Lieutenant-Colonel Burr, wished to act on the defensive; but as the message required him to move down and attack the Peishwa's army, he immediately sent the 2nd battalion, 6th regiment, to protect the stores, ammunition and followers in the village of Kirkee, left his camp standing, and instantly marched down by the high road for about a mile; then wheeling to the right, he moved in the direction of Dápooree to facilitate junction with Captain Ford's corps, and bring his front parallel to that of the enemy. In a few minutes the expected corps was seen approaching; the Resident's party had joined it, and Colonel Burr advanced to the attack. The Mahrattas, who had sent

5

on their skirmishers, some of whom had already suffered from the fire of the light infantry, were surprised by this forward movement in troops who they had been encouraged to believe were already spiritless; and a damp, which had been spreading over the whole army by the accidental breaking of the staff of the "Juree Putka," or Mahratta Standard, before they left the city, was now much increased. Gôklá, with the true spirit of a soldier, was riding from rank to rank, animating, encouraging and taunting as he thought most effectual; but the Peishwa's heart failed him, and after the troops had advanced, he sent a message to Gôklá, desiring him, "to be sure not to fire the first gun." At this moment the British troops were halted, their guns were unlimbering,—it was the pause of preparation and of anxiety on both sides; but Gôklá, observing the messenger from the Peishwa, and suspecting the nature of his errand, instantly commenced the attack by opening a battery of nine guns, detaching a strong corps of rocket-camels to the right, and pushing forward his cavalry to the right and left. The British troops were soon nearly surrounded by horse; but the Mahratta infantry, owing to this rapid advance, were left considerably in the rear, except a regular battalion under a Portuguese named De Pinto, which had marched by a shorter route, (concealed for a time under cover of the enclosures,) and were now forming, with apparent steadiness, immediately in front of the 1st battalion, 7th regiment, and the grenadiers of the 2nd battalion, 6th. No sooner, however, were their red coats and colours exposed to view of the English sepoys, than the latter, with one accord, pushed forward to close, and, in their eagerness, got detached from the rest of the line. Gôklá, hoping that they might either be disposed to come over, or that he might be able to take advantage of their impetuosity, prepared a select body of 6,000 horse, which accompanied by the "Juree Putka," and headed by several persons of distinction, had been held in reserve near his left, these were now ordered to charge. The Mahratta guns ceased firing to let them pass; and they came down at speed, in a diagonal direction across the British front. Giving their fire, and receiving that of the line, they rode right at the 7th. Colonel Burr was the first to perceive the moving mass; he had just time to stop the pursuit of De Pinto's battalion, already routed, and to call to the men, who could not be dressed in line, to reserve their fire, and prove themselves worthy of all his care. Fortunately there was a deep slough, of which neither party was aware, immediately in front of the British left. The foremost of the horses rolled over, and many, before they could be pulled up, tumbled over those in front; the fire, hitherto reserved, was now given with great effect, numbers fell, the confusion became extreme, and the force of the charge was completely checked: a very small proportion came in contact with the bayonets, a few continued the attack in the rear, but many turned back; some galloped round the left as if to plunder tne camp, but they were driven off by a few shots from two iron guns at Kirkee, and the sepoys had nearly repulsed the attack before a company of Europeans could arrive to their support. This failure completely disconcerted the Mahrattas; they began to drive off their guns; their infantry retired from the distant position they occupied, and upon the advance of the British line the whole field was cleared. The brigade returned to its position at Kirkee after nightfall, and the light battalion and auxiliary horse joined it next morning. The report of their arrival, and the effect of the forward movement, deterred Gôklá from renewing the attack. The Mahrattas in Captain Ford's battalion deserted, and a part of the newly raised auxiliary horse were, at their own desire, permitted to quit the British camp; but not one sepoy of the regular service left his colours. The number of the British troops engaged at the affair of Kirkee, including Captain Ford's battalion, was 2,800 rank and file, of whom about 800 were Europeans. Their loss was comparatively trifling, amounting only to 86 men in killed and wounded, 50 of whom were of the sepoys on the left. The Mahratta army consisted of 18,000 horse and 8,000 foot with 14 guns. They suffered considerably, having lost 500 men in killed and wounded; and though the proportion of horses killed on the spot was inconsiderable, a very great number were disabled. Amongst the slain was the minister, Móró Dixit, who, by a strange fatality, was mortally wounded by a grape-shot from one of the guns attached to the battalion of his friend Captain Ford.

Hostilities were no sooner commenced than the ferocious

and vindictive character of Bájee Rao's previous orders became apparent from the proceedings in every direction, probably before he had time to stop them. The Residency was plundered and burnt, and of the Resident's library and private apartments not one stone was left upon another; the families and followers of the troops who fell into the hands of the Mahrattas were robbed, beaten and frequently mutilated; gardens were destroyed, trees were torn from the roots, and graves dug up. An engineer officer on survey was attacked and killed; two brothers of the name of Vaughan, one of them a captain in the Madras army, were taken while travelling between Bombay and Poona, near the village of Tullygaom, and though they made no resistance, were most barbarously hanged under the superintendence of a Bráhmin, named Bábjee Punt Gôklá.

As soon as General Smith found the communication cut off, he advanced on Poona. From the time his division quitted Seroor he was followed by flying parties of Mahrattas who, owing to his want of cavalry, harassed his march. He arrived on the evening of the 13th, and preparations were made to attack the Peishwa before daylight of the 15th, whose army, having obtained a considerable addition by the junction of most of the southern jagheerdars (chiefs), had come out a few days before, and encamped with its left on the late cantonment of the British troops, and its right stretching along the Hyderabad road for several miles. The intended attack, however, on the morning of the 15th was postponed by General Smith in consequence of unforeseen difficulties at the ford.

About sunset on the evening of the 16th an advanced brigade was ordered to cross the ford, and take up a position to the east of the Peishwa's army, at the village of Ghôre-puray, for the purpose of co-operating in an intended attack on the ensuing morning. It was opposed by a body of the Peishwa's infantry, supported by parties of horse and two guns; but having succeeded in getting to its station, though with the loss of 84 men in killed and wounded, it was no longer molested during the night. In the morning, when General Smith moved towards the Mahratta camp, he found it abandoned, and that the Peishwa had fled towards Sátára. During the day the city was surrendered, and the greatest care being taken, on this, as on every occasion, by General Smith for the protection of the peaceable part of the community, order and tranquillity were soon re-established. General Smith remained at Poona for five days, during which time communication with Bombay was opened, and a party being detached for the purpose, succeeded in capturing several guns in the neighbourhood of the fort of Singurh. Some of the inhabitants of Poona, who fled, as usual, with their property towards the hill-forts, were sufferers on this occasion, as a great quantity of baggage was taken with the guns, and became the booty of the army.

General Smith left Poona on the 22nd November in hot pursuit of Bájee Rao, who fled round by Máholee, Punderpoor, to Báhmunwarree near Joonere, where Trimbuckjee Dainglià joined him with reinforcements, after having stockaded all the passes in that very strong country. Pressed again by General

Smith the Peishwa doubled back towards Poona, but passing the City by, hurried along the Ahmednuggur road with the probable intention of surprising the British Station of Seroor, or at least of intercepting reinforcements on the way at Poona.

One such reinforcement, 500 infantry, 2 guns and 300 irregular horse under Captain Staunton, were on the road, and on New Year's morning, 1818, after a long night march, were descending to the village of Korygaum to cross the Bheema, when Bájee Rao's army with 25,000 cavalry and 6,000 foot, were descried on the opposite bank. Captain Staunton instantly threw himself into the half-fortified village, which his handful of troops held all day and night without food, almost without water, surrounded on all sides, and constantly engaged in hand-to-hand conflicts with Arabs and Pathans, who effected a lodgement in the very heart of the village. Bájee Rao was a spectator from a safe distance, the Rájá of Sátára was there also, and Trimbuckjee Dainglià, who twice entered the village sword in hand; the while Bájee Rao taunted Gôklá and his other generals—"Where were now their boasts of defeating the English when they could not overcome one battalion?" At nine o'clock on the morning of the end, having lost 500 men, Bájee Rao decamped and fled hot foot to the South, pursued by General Pritzler; while Captain Staunton returned to Seroor, having lost 175 out of his 500 infantry and artillery, while 100 out of his 300 cavalry were killed, wounded, or missing, and two-thirds of the British officers were killed or wounded.

Bájee Rao in his flight southward hoped to reach and get

aid and shelter from the Rájá of Mysore, but he nearly ran into the arms of General Munro, doubled back again over the Sálpee Ghaut and away beyond Shôlapoor. Generals Smith and Pritzler then joined forces to take up the pursuit, but Mr. Elphinstone formed another plan, and sent one of these armies to reduce all the forts in both the Deccan and Kônkan, another to hunt down Bájee Rao.

The Governor-General, incensed by Bájee Rao's treachery, had determined at last to terminate the Bráhmin dynasty, and wisely gave Mr. Elphinstone *carte blanche* to settle the country as seemed to him good. On the details of the organisation and system by which this able administrator reduced anarchy and chaos to stable government, we need not dwell; but will follow Bájee Rao as he fled north to seek protection from Hôlkar and Sindia, aye, even from the very Pindarrees! Hôlkar this time was already first in the field, and Sindia held back, so Sir Thomas Hislop attacked and completely routed the former at Seeprah on 21st December. After this victory Sindia saw the error of his ways, and the British troops were free to annihilate the Pindárrees under that picturesque freebooter, Cheetoo, who was soon after killed by a tiger below Asseergurh. Sir Thomas Hislop then marched south to find Bájee Rao, who, too late for Hôlkar's rising, had turned back to Chándore. The Peishwa had scarcely arrived there when, in panic at Hislop's advance, he bolted to Kôpergaum; thence again, finding General Smith approaching him from the south, he rushed off to Chándah in the territory of the Nâgpoor Bhônslay, but Mr. Jenkins, the

Resident, sent out a force and turned him back at the river Wardah where he was headed at every point by British detachments. His brother Chimnájee and two of his best generals then fled south and gave themselves up to General Smith. Many of his chiefs and Sirdars deserted, until at last Bájee Rao was left alone with 8,000 men headed hy the loyal chiefs Vinchoorhar and Poorandharee, He had already sent many messages to Mr. Elphinstone offering to treat—absurd proposals which the latter would not notice: he now addressed himself to his old friend Sir John Malcolm at Mhow. Sir John sent out Lieutenant (afterwards Sir John) Low to negotiate, and after much palaver Bájee Rao surrendered his sword to that officer (3rd June, 1818), renounced his sovereignty, bound himself to retire for good to Bithoor, and to give up Trimbuckjee Dainglià, on condition of his being granted the enormous pension of eight lakhs of rupees per annüm. The Marquis of Hastings ratified the promise with great reluctance, notwithstanding that Bájee Rao failed to surrender Trimbuckjee Dainglià, who, however, was soon after caught in Khándeish, and imprisoned for life in Bengal.

Bájee Rao was conducted to Bithoor and there died, having previously adopted a youth of a respectable Chitpáwan Bráhmin family of Sungamèshwar in the Kônkan, whose memory is execrated by the human race as the demon Náná Sahèb of Cawnpoor.

Thus ended—for ever—the Bráhmin dynasty of Poona. The City knew Bájee Rao no more; but the City of the

Peishwas afterwards received his emissaries, has often harboured those of his descendants, has undoubtedly been visited by the accursed Náná Sahèb, certainly prior to the mutiny, probably and not unfrequently, since he was proscribed. His venom was of the viscid tenacious kind, it has adhered to certain of his caste fellows, and ever and anon —as now—produces hideous secondary diseases of the mind.

Bájee Rao had not one redeeming point in his character: he had no natural instincts of family affection—he had no bowels of mercy—he had no religious feeling, though he was intensely superstitious. He never had a friend or ally but at some time or other he betrayed, or sacrificed him —he did not know what gratitude meant. He never made a promise or swore an oath that he did not break it—he never entered into a treaty or an agreement that he did not, while he signed, think how he might evade it. He was conceited as a peacock, but feeble at a crisis as a worm—he roared like a lion, but he ran away like a hare. He never told the truth, even by accident, or to himself. He trusted no one, and, in the worst sense, never let his left hand know what his right hand was doing. Rapacious and miserly as Harpagon, he was yet lavish and reckless in his licentiousness, and even more depraved than Casanova. All the worst attributes of Ahab, Jezebel, Ananias and Judas Iscariot were combined in him. In very truth he was an incarnation of evil such as is difficult to be found in the history of mankind. Even the Poona patriots of the present day have hesitated to make a hero of him!

Mr. Mountstuart Elphinstone remained at Poona for another year, during which he not only settled all the troubles of the great chiefs, rewarded substantially all private persons who had cast in their lot with the British, and pensioned others, but also introduced excellent Revenue, Judicial, Civil and Criminal Codes. On 1st November, 1819, he became Governor of Bombay, leaving behind him in Máháráshtra a reputation for honour, humanity, righteous and generous dealing, foresight and sagacity which has never been equalled and never will be effaced.

For thirty-seven years, from 1820 to 1857, the history of Poona presents no stirring incidents, but the citizens, daily increasing in numbers and prosperity, enjoyed peace and protection of their lives and property such as had never before been experienced. The City was the first to reap the benefits of railway communication, but before a steam engine ran into the cantonment the great Mutiny broke out, and Poona became the focus of all discontent and intrigue. It was not the citizens, however, who busied themselves with sedition, *they* were generally well disposed, it was the emissaries from the north-west, from Central India and the Carnatic, who used the City as their meeting-place. Held in a vice, however, by the prudent military dispositions of Lord Elphinstone, the City passed with comparative ease through the terrible ordeal of 1857—58. The Iron Horse soon brought in more population; and Poona, till the completion of the Bhore Ghaut incline and the prolongation of the Great Indian Peninsular Railway towards Madras, flourished as the chief centre of the Deccan.

In 1860 Sir Bartle Frere came, and with innate taste transformed the suburbs. Rich Bombay citizens built country houses, and cast about for investments of surplus capital in the Deccan. Palatial barracks were erected, roads made in every direction, the river Moota was dammed back and Lake Fife soon poured water round the City, till it is surrounded by sugar cane and highly cultivated gardens. The native industries in silver, brass, copper and iron revived; gold thread and lace factories and carpet weaving were soon followed by paper and sugar mills, by distilleries and breweries.

The City itself, originally laid out with some method in Peiths or streets, many named after deities and the days of the week, drained into the Moota River, and will so drain until the Government relieve a Bráhmin-ridden, ignorant and self-sufficient municipality of its powers. Poona City, sufficiently supplied with good water, not over-crowded, enjoying a good climate, ought to be the healthiest, not one of the dirtiest of Deccan towns.

Poona City, like many other towns, has had its riots, its incendiary conflagrations, its robberies and dacoities during the past 20 years: it has just had its Jubilee murders. All these evils have been the work of a handful of malcontents and of "Cranks" whose movements have unwisely been disregarded by the Powers that be. The people of Poona, as history proves and we shall yet see, are timorous and industrious, peaceable and law abiding—they only want governing—*not* by Bráhmins!

## CHAPTER V.

### THE POONA AND DECCAN PRESS.

THERE can be no greater mistake, no greater injustice than to stigmatise the whole Vernacular and Anglo-Vernacular Press of Western India as disloyal. The whole of the *Bombay* Native Press, all the Guzeráthi, and, with a few exceptions, all the Mahommedan newspapers are sound and healthy, are fair and temperate, if sometimes mistaken in their criticism of Governmental measures, and British administration. They are also moderately considerate, and sometimes in the right, when they take individuals to task. They do not always throw mud recklessly in the hope that some of it may stick to the white man's face. They usually refrain from malicious comments on social questions or incidents that they do not understand. In this respect, indeed, they contrast favourably with many Society Journals in England. This may be gall and wormwood to many of my readers, more especially to Anglo-Indians, but it is strictly true. *C'est moi qui le dit!* No official has been at once more fairly criticised, more foully libelled than the writer.

The faults of the Native Press consist, *first of all*, and

of course, in ignorance, inexperience, and a want of breadth of view; *secondly*, in their credulity—they habitually fail to distinguish between fact and mere rumour, are prone to accept as authentic, and to publish without enquiry, any wild tale, or, as it is termed in India, any piece of "gup" that seems likely to interest their readers and increase their circulation. *Thirdly*, they are not over particular in their selection of matter to fill their columns so long as their columns are filled, for they have not many trustworthy contributors of original matter, nor could they afford to pay them if they existed. How many dozen London journals are there with whom the same faults might be found, but who have not the same excuse?

On the other hand there are several Vernacular and Anglo-Vernacular papers in Bombay and up country, which can give points to hundreds of London and Provincial papers; Mr. Malábari's weekly "Spectator", for instance, "Native Opinion", "The Rást-Goftar"—they have always been good, and every year they are becoming better and setting good examples to the Native Press generally. It is an insult to them to confound them with the Reptile Press of the Deccan.

The seditionmongers of the Deccan—the Poona, Sátára, Wai rattlesnakes—have hatched out on the Congress dung-heap within the past quarter of a century; prior to 1875 they can hardly be said to have existed. Even when Lord Lytton, irritated by the licentiousness of the Calcutta Baboo Press, unwisely passed his "Gagging Act", the tone of the then not numerous journals of Máháráshtra was not very objectionable. But the Congress, fostered by the only weak Viceroy India has ever had, aided if not invented by one of his secretaries and another hare-brained secretary in Bombay, sprang into life; forthwith the malcontents at the capital of the Peishwas—young men who could not qualify for Government employ, who failed to effect an entrance by the back door of interest, who owed their free education to Government Colleges—saw their opportunity. It does not require much capital to start a native press—a thousand rupees goes a long way. The countless petty Chiefs and Sirdars were easily cajoled into subscribing to any scurrilous sheet under the pretext that they were aiding the Congress movement *which the Viceroy approved of*—or if they held aloof, they were vilified and their administration attacked mercilessly. They one and all gave in, and blackmail was the backbone of Native Press finance. The history of the "Scourge of the Deccan" which follows, is nearly the exact history of the "Mahratta" newspaper whose proprietor and editor, a previous Member of Lord Sandhurst's Legislative Council, already once imprisoned for libel has just been sentenced for seditious writings.

I have written (*vide* St. James' Gazette, 30th June) that the Marquis of Ripon is mainly responsible: other writers have said the same. To justify the allegation it is only necessary to go back to 1857, the year of the Mutiny, and 1858, the demise of Good John Company, and to pass in review the Proconsuls who have since presided over the destinies of the Bombay Presidency.

We thus prepare this Chart. In it we trace without difficulty the growth of the gangrene in the Deccan, and can measure its dimensions. To use Sam Weller's words with reference to the fascinating "Smangle" in the Fleet—"The late prevailance of a close and confined atmosphere has been rather favourable to the growth of veeds of an alarmin' and sangvinary nature; but with that 'ere exception things is quiet enough." The exception, however, becomes serious for India when the "veeds" are found thriving not only in the Poona Council Hall, but in special English newspapers, in the very chambers of the House of Commons, of the India Office, on the shelves of the India Office Library, and—incredible though it may seem—in the British Museum Reading Room. The Powers that be incur a heavy responsibility by hesitating to cleanse Public Offices of this "alarmin' and sangvinary growth."

As to the seditious native press of Poona and the Deccan generally, it suffices to note that inasmuch as the Penal Code has at last been proved sufficiently comprehensive to deal with it, no new laws or restrictions are needed. Vigilance is all that is called for.

# TEMPERATURE CHART OF THE NATIVE POONA PRESS, 1857 TO 1897.

**PATIENT'S NAME AND ADDRESS.**

Dùshtee Rao, Pâjee, Bàncootekar * B. A., J. P.

Member of the Legislative Council of Bombay.

Editor and Proprietor of the "Jootkari" and "The Scourge."

**FORMER ADDRESS:** Government House or Council Hall, Poona; or, Shanwár Peith, Poona City.

**PRESENT OR FUTURE ADDRESS:** Uncertain.

**GOVERNORS OF BOMBAY.**

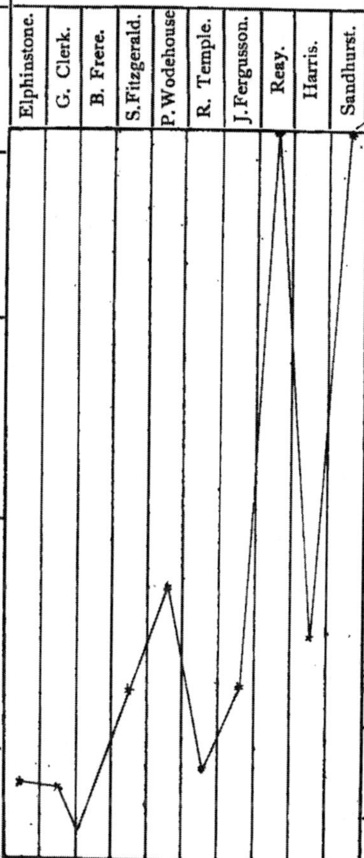


| Annas in Rupee. | TREATMENT. |
|---|---|
| Blood 18 an. * | Eau de luce mixt. Leg. Council draught, by Lord Sandhurst. |
| Fever 16 an. | Government House Alcohol in large doses, with rancid butter by Lord Reay. |
| Bubbling 10 an. | Sleeping draught, by Sir P. Wodehouse. Iced Water, by Lord Harris. Palm Oil, by Sir S. Fitzgerald. |
| Smoke 6 an. | Cold Water, by Sir J. Fergusson. |
| Steam 4 an. | Hot fomentation, by Sir R. Temple. |
| Normal 1 an. | Zinc Ointment, by Sir G. Clerk. Cold Cream, by Lord Elphinstone. |
| Zero 0 | Vaseline, by Sir B. Frere. |

**Remarks by Matron Britannia, July 1897.** The patient has suffered from the irritants exhibited by Lords Reay and Sandhurst, and needs firm, resolute treatment, and constant watching. MARY BRITAIN.

**FUTURE TREATMENT.** Cautery. Perhaps an operation. Anti-Congress Pills.
G. HAMILTON,
*Ind. Office: Resdt. Surgeon.*

**Visiting Surgeon, or Medical Board, or Inspector-General.** Dr. G. H's treatment approved as proposed.—Why was it not adopted sooner?
JOHN BULL, *Inspector General.*

* '*Dushtee*' treacherous; '*Pâjee*' bad character; '*Bancoote*' modern Bánkôt.

## CHAPTER VI.

### THE "SCOURGE OF THE DECCAN."

THE scene opens in "Shanwár Peith" or Saturday Street, Poona, where reside philosophers, editors of mighty daily and weekly journals, the local "Pottses" and "Slagges" (*vide* Pickwick) of the Deccan. A handsome young Bráhmin of the highest caste is seen descending carefully from a ricketty "pony-shigram", the "growler" of the city of the Peishwas. His clean-cut features, his arched black eyebrows, with small, well-waxed moustache to match—his forehead clean shaven (the holy caste-mark fresh as paint in the centre above his nose) surmounting a pair of small green-grey eyes, with intelligence and craft in every glance—a valuable pearl in the lobe of each ear—his head-gear a handsome but somewhat large turban of soft grass-green material of many folds, its "kincob" fringe modestly peeping out at the curved peak—a valuable cashmere shawl of the same hue, folded carefully, but seemingly worn carelessly, over his left shoulder—a white calico jacket, wrinkled and extremely tight from elbow to wrist—his "dhotur" made of delicate salmon-pink muslin, with broad phylactery gracefully folded, forming, as it were, richly

OFFICE OF THE "SCOURGE OF THE DECCAN", SHANWÁR PEITH OR SATURDAY STREET, POONA

*(See pages 87—88.)*

broidered Zouâve-like "knickerbockers" (if one may dare so to call them), descending to the knees and passing deftly between his legs, brought tightly round his waist, and again *tucked in* (Again! "Mâf karâ Máhárâj!"—Forgive me, my Lord!) so as to end in a broad flat terminal, decently falling in front. Below the knees—alas! below the knees!—this decidedly picturesque bravery terminates in long, white, cotton stockings, baggy, wrinkled and ill-fitting by reason of the wearer's somewhat deficient calves—the great climax being reached by splay feet *plunged* (I can find no fitter term) into patent leather *ankle jacks* with elastic sides, of which the tags protruding offensively behind.

Surely this is some great chief "incog."? No, my readers. Hear his full title—Rao Sahèb (*self-dubbed*) Vinkatèsh Mhâdeo Phoolmándikar—commonly called "Bábá Sahèb"—educated at Yerrowda College—Bachelor of Arts of the Bombay University—aspirant for a fat post in the Political Department; *par exemple*, the Agency or Tutorship to a minor Mahratta Chief, where there is little to do (but intrigue, of course) and plenty to get—with a Fellowship, a Rao Báhádurship, Membership of the Legislative Council, and "Paramèshwar" (God) only knows what further honours looming in the distance.

This is what your true new Bráhmin loves and aims at—these are the goals which a few only have reached by hard work, zeal, and means more fair than foul.

"Bábá Sahèb" thinks his chances good, he is believed in his own circle, and he really believes himself, to stand high in favour at Government House. But if Captain and Rissaldar Major No-bât Khán, the native aide-de-camp who receives him with a covert smile and sends in his private card to the "Pryvit Sahèb" (Private Secretary), would only tell what he knows!!—If the "Pryvit Sahèb" could tell, who reads his name with curses not loud but deep, and orders him to be ushered in, simply because he knows if he does not see him then, he will come again next day, and next day, and next, till he obtains admission. It is nothing that it is English mail day, and the "Pryvit Sahèb" is writing for dear life—this bore must be seen first, treated patiently and got rid of, or what would Mr. Abel say?—And the globe-trotter, sucking in lies from an eminent Congress-walla in the cosy guest-room upstairs, what would *he* say? Are not our Aryan brethren to be treated "with the utmost consideration?" (*Vide* Secretary of State's despatch—I forget the number of it.) So the poor "Pryvit Sahèb" throws down his pen in despair—composes his face into a ghastly smile—wheels round his chair, says to the scarlet and gold Peon in attendance, "Anè do (Let him come in)—d—n—ahem! I mean, bless him", and the sacrifice is duly accomplished!!

If "Pryvit Sahèbs" could only divulge their experiences! If Mr. G. W. H. R. H. would only publish all he suffered in days gone-by, the book would be as fascinating as "Greville's Memoirs."

But to return to the fascinating Bábá Sahèb!

We left him on the narrow pathway in Shanwár Peith.

He stops before a small white-washed house of one upper floor, whence projects a narrow wooden balcony. painted

THE SECRET COMPACT.
INTERIOR OF THE EDITOR'S ROOM OF THE "SCOURGE OF THE DECCAN."

bright green, architecture decidedly modern Bráhminical. The lower part of this enticing dwelling is nearly covered by a huge sign-board—blue ground, white letters—announc ing in Mahratti above and in English below (patriotic this, we observe!) that this is "*The Office of 'The Scourge of the Deccan.*'"—(Appropriate title, by the way!) A somewhat dilapidated box with one sound, one broken hinge, and no lock worth mentioning, but coloured green (one coat, from the paint left over from the balcony)—depends from a rusty nail in the door-post. Bábá Sahèb, taking his turban off carefully, stumbles up a break-neck staircase, makes a peculiar knock at a low door on the landing, bearing a paper notice "*Editor's Room. Private.*" It is speedily unlocked by an unkempt, dissipated-looking, dirty and somewhat highly flavoured individual—naked to the waist—soiled, once white cotton stockings tumbling about his ankles, bare-headed and shaven, except as to the whisp of hair on his crown; which whisp, by the way, a friend of mine accustomed to Hindoo clerks, declares he never can see let down without his fingers itching to take a pull at it! This charming creature, a Deccan Bráhmin by his forehead marks, is Mr. Vishnu Parashram, alias Bhow Sahèb, the gifted Editor of "*The Scourge of the Deccan!*"

The two heroes salute "more Brahminico", while they enter the room where Bhow Sahèb makes up his scourges, and also apparently drinks strong drinks—for, lo! a half-empty whisky bottle and a glass on a ricketty table, and several "dead men" rolled into a corner with empty soda-water bottles labelled in Mahratti "*Pure Bráhmin manufacture.*" The windows have probably not been opened since they were blown in last monsoon. The room absolutely reeks of spirits, stale "hubble-bubble" smoke, and other foul human odours. From the atmosphere and Bhow Sahèb's appearance there can be no doubt he was beastly drunk last night!

What a contrast between the two men! Bábá Sahèb I have already described. The other is short, beetle-browed, bandy-legged, evil-looking, with ferret-like, beady, black eyes that throw malicious glances as he speaks. Hollow-chested, tormented by a hacking cough, again and again he wipes great drops of cold perspiration from his brow on to the floor, with the back of his trembling hand.

Son of a low-born "koolkarni" (village accountant) in an obscure village near Shôlapur—his father had managed to establish a claim of Rs. 10 monthly on the hereditary Patell (Head-man) of his village—blackmail to keep him silent regarding some villainy they had perpetrated together. With this money Bhow Sahèb had been clothed, scantily fed and educated (free) at the great Government school in Shôlapur City. Developing considerable ability he gained a small Scholarship, and then another. Thenceforward his path was clear—Yerrowda College—another Scholarship with a fair prospect of a University career; but Bhow, alas! fell into evil courses at Yerrowda. Relying for his pocket-money on wages earned by writing letters for ignorant people, he took to higher flights and was at last detected and expelled for sending anonymous letters.

Leaving his poor father broken-hearted (for he loved him

dearly despite his faults—the old man did!), he went to Bombay where he speedily became well known in the purlieus of all the Government Offices as a good man for concocting anonymous letters and petitions. Associating with the reporters of the Reptile Vernacular Press, he was employed as an agent to obtain Government information surreptitiously. Time went on. Bhow Sahèb was 27 years old when a secret and highly important despatch from the Bombay Government to the Viceroy somehow found its way into the Native Press. Inquiry followed, and suspicion pointed to Bhow Sahèb. Escaping from a Police Warrant, he hid himself about the temples of that hellish town Pundapur; keeping up, however, secret correspondence with, and mildly blackmailing, his old friends of the Vernacular Press, and contributing "leading articles" and lies, for which he was well paid.

Halcyon days then fell upon him. The National Congress sprang to existence from the seething mud of discontent and disloyalty. One of its leaders saw his way to a good thing. Thought he, "Establish a rattling Anglo-Vernacular in the Capital of the Deccan, with capital, part cash down, part promised by terrified Chiefs and Rájáhs. Force the circulation by publishing all the scandals, social and otherwise, to be gathered against Englishmen in India; let there be no white face but shall be spotted with the mud we shall throw—some of it will stick! Fool Mr. A. O. H., Sir W. W., Mr. C. and others of the hated race to the top of their bent. Interfere everywhere and foment discord everywhere.

So shall *I* gain notoriety and rupees pour into *my* pockets!" In exactly this way were at least a dozen Poona papers started, some of which flickered for a few years like the numerous exhalations over a pestilential swamp, and then died out. Half a dozen or so remain, like the "*Mahratta*," the "Vaibhow" and the "*Kesári*."

At such a crisis an able editor was naturally needed, and who so fit as Bhow Sahèb, the daring, the unscrupulous, the able writer then on the spot in Poona City? Terms were arranged, the mansion in Shanwàr Peith engaged, and in due course came out the "Scourge of India," causing no little sensation by the audacity, insolence, and disloyalty of its tone towards the Government, and its scurrilous imputations against all English gentlemen and ladies within reach. The circulation was considerable for several years; and Bhow Sahèb, receiving a handsome salary, lived like a fighting cock, but unfortunately for his health, also drank like a fish. The native Chiefs and Rájáhs paid up regularly, or were forced to do so by threats of exposure of mismanagement of their estates. The proprietor became quite a power in the Western Presidency, bought himself shares in several good cotton mills, invested in a "*Lust garten*" or pleasure-garden in the country near Poona, and all went merry as the marriage bells!

But the reaction after delay—sickening to English minds—set in. The Congress itself began to flag, and, what was of more importance, not to pay its way, despite strenuous endeavours to revivify it by the importation of strange

Presidents for the annual meetings. Naturally the Reptile Press, especially the Vernacular portion of it, was affected—Chiefs and Rájáhs "humped their backs" and swore they would submit to this tyranny no longer. Serious prosecutions of, and heavy sentences on, native editors followed. Sedition and scurrilous writing received a crushing blow, and many of the mushroom papers disappeared for the time into outer darkness, till silly Governors shed reays (I mean rays) of encouragement on the native Press.

Now it is needless to say that a grandee like Bábá Sahèb, did not seek the Editor of the "Scourge of the Deccan" for nothing! There happened to be at the moment a vacancy pending in the tutorship of the young Maharajah of Trickapore, which Bábá Sahèb had applied for and believed he would get. He desired the support of the Vernacular Press which (it was then in the halycon days aforesaid) the Government of the day actually placed faith in! He came therefore to Bhow Sahèb whom he had known at the College, to secure such aid as he would give in the valuable columns of the "Scourge of the Deccan." Bhow Sahéb, on the other hand, was glad to see him because he, too, thought that Bábá Sahèb, influential as he was with many leading men connected with the Congress, might be able to help him to secure a better paid post, or at any rate, an increase of salary where he was. A conversation then ensued between this worthy pair, which I will briefly relate; but first of all I must make a small digression.

People in England are apt to confuse the educated Indians

they see from India, and discern no difference between the polished, self-possessed and comparatively modest Bráhmin, and the impudent, self-assertive Baboo from Calcutta. "They are all Indians," and that is all they think about it! We, in Western India, however, know better. Our educated Bráhmins do *not* misquote Shakespeare and Shelley, or use poluphlosboic polysyllables in converse with each other. They speak, on the contrary, fairly good and well-chosen English, and are not to be contaminated by Baboodom. Talking of Baboodom, I am given to understand, that a Committee has been formed at the India Office for compiling the new language which the great spread of education in Bengal, and the large influx of Baboos into London has rendered necessary. "Baboonese," the new language is called! The Committee is composed of Sir G. Goodbird, Mr. Protest, a well-known retired Bombay professor, and the talented author of those amusing Baboo papers that recently appeared in "Punch". Up to the present the Committee are chagrined to find that the language lacks even the rudiments of grammar, but there is abundant material for a Baboonese "phrase-dictionary" which accordingly will soon be "announced by the Press."

To proceed. * Quoth Bhow Sahèb to Bàbà Sahèb, "You have not been near me to see me for some time past, and I was afraid I had offended you."

"Oh no," replied Bàbà Sahèb, "you have always been

* The enunciation is difficult to render. It is distinct, each syllable being separately pronounced.

present in my heart, and you know that the other day in a speech I made at the Congress I specially lauded the 'Scourge' and its talented Editor.—Well, to be quite frank," continued Bábá Sahèb, "I want you in return to do me a little favour now. There is that tutorship at Trickapore soon to be vacant—I have applied for it, and with 'Ishwur's' (God's) and your help I have every hope of obtaining it. Now see here—let's make a bargain. *You* put in your next issue a nice sugary little paragraph in my favour about this same appointment, and *I* will undertake to do my best with the Secretaries of the Congress to give you a good turn. What do you say, eh?"

"Agreed!" said Bhow Sahèb; "'done with you' as they say at the Poona races."

Here Bábá Sahèb picked up his turban, and while carefully readjusting it on his head, observed, "I say, Bhow Sahèb, "what in Shaitan's name is that leading article you seem to be racking your brains over?"

"Well," said Bhow Sahèb, "it is causing me too much annoyance—it is about the recent appointment to the Council. It seems to me to be the great job which has never been properly exposed and condemned by any Vernacular Press, and I was just putting finishing touch when you came in."

"Ah! my friend," said Bábá Sahèb, "you must not put your finishing touches. Your finishing touches will be not worth much if you go on drinking so much whisky as I see you are doing. Have some! *What! I?* Not for a lakh of

THE SNAKE'S PROGRESS (WITH APOLOGIES TO HOGARTH).
(*See page 98.*)

rupees! As for your article about that appointment, just take my advice, put it in waste-paper basket. It cannot be worth much if you composed it yesterday, old friend—besides, let me tell you, you are altogether wrong—that appointment is very good one, as good as could have been made, and I will sum the whole question up by a little joke, which I thought to send to the Editor of *Punch*, but will now present to you. Why is the latest appointment to the Bombay Council eminently satisfactory? Give it up, eh? Because all parties concerned, Secretary of State, Lord Sandhurst and the person nominated, has each got 'Oll-e-vant' (Ollivant). Samajla ka?" (Vulg. "Do you twig?")

With these words he saluted Bhow Sahèb jauntily, and tumbled downstairs as well as he could into the street.

When he had again locked the door Bhow Sahèb sat him down to think, and very bitter indeed were the thoughts that passed through his mind. Here was this young whipper-snapper coming to deride him and give him advice, while at the same time he wanted him to do him a favour! "This is not to be endured. However, I will keep my promise, and give him right good smack on back besides." With that Bhow Sahèb, fortifying himself with a stiff glass of "the dog that bit him," sat down and indited, first, one short editorial notice about the vacancy at Trickapore, in which he lauded Bábá Sahèb, and pressed his claim to the skies. Next he wrote a long leading article against pushing young natives generally, and headed it—"Prevalence of 'Khatpat' (Intrigue) at Government House."

To have done with Bhow Sahèb—I may mention that in a few months phthisis and delirium tremens combined, brought him to a miserable end.

And now for Bábá Sahèb. Finding himself in the street, he assumed his most dignified air, while he hesitated in which direction he should bend his steps. He was really due at a High Festival on the top of Parbuttee, * but it was very hot and a good three miles' "shigram" drive; on the other hand, he could easily stroll down to the Hiria Bâgh (Garden) in the shade of the houses, and there, in a little temple close by, go through such religious ceremonies as were still expected from him, though he did not believe a jot in them himself. Accordingly he bent his steps southward, with slow and dignified mien. Many a casement and shutter were slyly opened, and bright female faces with jewelled nose-rings were pressed cautiously forward, that the owner might admire the well-known youth as he passed. As he got into the smaller and more populated lanes, the respect shown to him and his sanctity as a "Chitpáwan" Bráhmin, became more marked at every step. The inferior castes, "Sudras" and the like, stood back against the walls and shops lest their foul shadows should fall on and defile him! The basket-women and vegetable sellers shuffled back into the road on their hams, dragging their

* A Temple on the top of Parbuttee Hill, where are also to be seen the blackened ruins of the palace of the infamous Bájee Rao, the last of the Peishwas. It was from there that Bájee Rao saw his great army defeated at Kirkee. The Jubilee murders were committed near the white house in the valley at the centre of this picture. (*See plate*, *p. 9.*)

baskets away for the same reason! Even the Máhommedan coffee-seller crying his wares, stopped short, open-mouthed, to gaze on the wonderful being. The very pariah dogs seemed to feel and fear his presence, and, if not forced to do so by sticks, slunk abashed down the nearest pathway.

A quiet evening, a little sensible reading, and Bábá Sahèb went to one of the numerous committees of which he was a member, where sedition was openly talked, and the downfall of the British freely predicted.

He will rise to be a great man, will Bábá Sahèb, as we shall see, for he moves and lives, is one of the most rising young natives in Poona City! and is ear-marked for the Legislative Council.

## CHAPTER VII.

### THE SIWAJEE REVIVAL.

THE so-called Siwajee Revival a few years ago was a remarkable circumstance which ought to have attracted the serious notice of the Bombay Government, seeing that it was got up by the Bráhmin press, by descendants of the very caste that for their own base ends and by the basest intrigues usurped the power of Siwajee's descendants. The most casual perusal of the history of Máháráshtra should have perceived that the Bráhmin enthusiasm was feigned, that their pretended patriotism was spurious and without doubt must be displayed with some sinister object, certainly inspired by feelings inimical to the British Ráj. Yet His Excellency the Governor—but, let us hope, *not* his Council—was smitten with admiration, and when a subscription was started to repair Siwajee's tomb or rather the platform on the summit of Raigurh Fort, on which his body was cremated, he eagerly gave his mite and thus expressed his sympathy with "a down-trod nation," his remarkable knowledge of Bráhminical character, his abhorrence of the neglect of English officials who had so long left the sacred masonry to crumble!

The subscription list must be of such historical value that it should be published, and the original, together with the account showing how much of the amounts promised were actually paid, should be deposited in the archives of the India Office! It would also be interesting to know what caused this touching outburst, why the Peishwa's caste

THE CREMATION PLATFORM OF SIWAJEE AT RAIGURH.

have forgotten for 300 years to restore the monument, or even to keep it in repair! Have they ever taken the trouble to recover from Mhár, the Bráhmin town at the foot of the fortress, the carved corner-stones, pillars and wood-work robbed from their hero's residence and Durbar halls to be built into the walls of the houses of the better classes, or into their cow-sheds?

The writer of these pages had the good fortune to visit Raigurh in the train of Sir Richard Temple during one of His Excellency's celebrated "Verification tours."

A mangy, ill-clad, highly flavoured old "poojaree" (worshipper) led us to what people call the tomb of Siwajee; an insignificant platform of decaying stones and mortar. We then proceeded to the "chowthara" or plinth—still in fair order—of the great Durbar hall in which it was Siwajee's wont to receive each year his various leaders, to distribute the spoil he and they had collected since last Dussera. The plinth faces east—Sir Richard mounted it, and we all stood around him while he made a heart-stirring recitation. I see the scene now vividly before my eyes—seem to hear his very words. He first described the wild Máwalis, and Hèdkaris and Pathans armed to the teeth, with shield, spear, sword and dagger, gathered in the Durbar hall and on the steps—bales of spoil scattered about—gold and silver—jewels—rich clothing—and cash galore. The great warrior Chiefs gathered in a semi-circle around the Founder of the Mahratta Empire, who, gorgeously arrayed, his good sword "Bhowânee" lying ready to his hand, sat on the kincob cushions of the throne, awarding praise or blame as seemed meet. A shortish, wiry man with looks of unusual intelligence, his visage generally displaying frank rough humour—his long ape-like arms (which Grant Duff tells us are thought a great beauty among the Mahratta race)—folded on his knees or held up in gesticulation. The whole scene mayhap was lit by the

SWAJEE'S NOCTURNAL DURBAR AT RAIGURH, AFTER THE SACK OF SURAT, JANUARY 6TH, 1664 A.D.

rays of the rising sun, dispelling the masses of fleecy clouds in the valleys beneath. Or, more likely still, a nocturnal Durbar lit up by waving torches, the back distance all in gloom, cross lights glinting off the polished shields and glittering spoil,—fierce faces appearing and disappearing—the tocsin resounding with enthusiastic cries of "Jèy! Siwajee Máháráj Jèy!" An embroidered "purdah" (curtain) stretched across the back of the hall, from which ever and anon peeped faces of the wives and female members of the family—exultant in the tumult. In the rear—fittest place for them—a few white-clad Bráhmins, like snakes in the grass—subservient, humble, treacherous, as was their wont.

"Anon," declaimed Sir Richard, "the scene changes. "The great Siwajee is dead and burnt on that plateau. It is the craven Sumbhajee, his son, who for the first time ascends his father's fortress, his mind filled with bloodthirsty intent, a discontented soldiery following him, presaging evil—with scant spoil to divide—the very crows and vultures seeming to scent blood in the air. The last surviving Queen-mother, Soyera Bye, has been deserted by all but Annaji Dutto and a few faithful adherents. The white-livered Bráhmins have long fled, and are endeavouring to make terms for themselves with the nearest party in power by the sale of secrets, by treachery of every kind. Soyera Bye is well-nigh alone when she is summoned to the ghastly Durbar, and foully abused by her stepson. Knowing that she has no chance of mercy, in her widow's weeds she ascends the 'chowthara,' and then with all the strength given to her at the supreme moment, she holds forth; the craven Sumbhajee the while, cowering on the throne his father has so recently occupied. 'Unworthy son of the great Siwajee', she screams, raising her shrivelled arm, 'if son thou art, which many doubt—I defy thee! Do thy worst! Thou comest hither, I know, for my blood and that of thy father's faithful servant: thou art now about to shed it. We die,'—raising both arms with clenched fists to heaven—'but may the wrath of the great Ishwar, may the curse of Bhowanee descend upon thee and thine!' No cries of 'Jey Sumbhajee' then, but a deadly gloom over the whole assemblage—a silence broken only by the guttural curses of the Máwalees and the clash of shields! *(See Plate page 19).*

"The Royal Widow, her face now veiled, is led away to execution, and the murderer seeks to drown his conscience and allay his fears by revelry and riot."

Sir Richard's declamation was magnificent, and he never faltered for a word.

The toil of ascent is at once forgotten by the marvellous beauty of the scenery when looking eastward from the "chowthára." Pertabghur in its majesty, Tôrna in its audacious lofty isolation, all the peaks bristling around Arthur's Seat, Elphinstone Point, the Saddleback and Mhyputghur in placid slumber, their summits touched by the last rays of the setting sun; their shadows dark purple, rosy edged, seem within a stone's throw—while the tiny stream of the infant Sávitree and its numerous petty tributaries glisten like silver threads as they wind about below.

On the further or eastern side of Pertabghur, in the valley between the Fort and Máhábuleswur, not far from where the travellers' bungalow now stands, is the site of the celebrated encounter between Siwajee and Áfzool Khán, the Môgul general.

In September 1659 the Beejapoor Government, incensed at Siwajee's successes, despatched Áfzool Khán, one of their best commanders, with 5,000 horse, 7,000 picked infantry and a strong train of artillery, rockets, and camel guns, to attack Siwajee in his stronghold. The force, owing to the rains, could not reach the Western Ghauts till October. Siwajee left Raigurh and went to Pertabghur to meet it; thence he despatched emissaries to the proud Môgul, pretending to be in great dread, expressing his contrition and beseeching Áfzool Khán's mediation for forgiveness. The latter, "vain as a Môgul" and despising "the mountain rat", sent a Bráhmin "wukeel", one of his staff, on from Waree to receive Siwajee's submission. Siwajee, after one or two interviews, visited the Bráhmin secretly in the dead of night and made this powerful appeal to him. "You are a Bráhmin, my superior in caste, my guide in religion! I tell you that all I have done has been for the sake of Hindoos and our Hindoo faith. The great Goddess Bhowanee herself has ordered me to protect Bráhmins and cattle, to slay these impious violators of your temples and your Gods, to resist the enemies of your religion. I call upon you, as a

Bráhmin, to help me to obey the Goddess's behests! Do this and you shall hereafter live here among your own caste, in your own country, in affluence, honoured above all Bráhmins."

Rich presents followed, and richer promises, and the Bráhmin envoy swore by all his gods to do anything that Siwajee might ask. A consultation followed at which Siwajee's confidential adviser, also a Bráhmin, assisted, when the Môgul's Envoy suggested that a vain man like his master, might be easily persuaded to meet Siwajee in friendly conference where he could be disposed of. Áfzool Khán fell into the trap, and consented to an interview at the foot of Pertabghur. Meantime Siwajee hurried up his trusty Máwulees by thousands and hid them in the jungles. Áfzool Khán, leaving the bulk of his army on the other side of Máhábuleshwur, came on with only fifteen hundred men, to within a few hundred yards of Pertabghur, where, at his Bráhmin Envoy's suggestion, they were halted "for fear of frightening Siwajee!" What followed is thus graphically told by Grant Duff.

"Áfzool Khán, a giant in stature, dressed in a thin muslin garment, armed only with his sword, and attended, as had been agreed, by a single armed follower, advanced in his palanquin to an open bungalow prepared for the occasion.

"Siwajee had made preparations for his purpose, not as if conscious that he meditated a criminal and treacherous deed, but as if resolved on some meritorious though desperate action. Having performed his ablutions with much earnestness, he laid his head at his mother's feet, and besought her blessing. He then arose, put on a steel chain cap and chain armour under his turban and cotton gown, concealed a crooked dagger, or 'beechwa' (literally, scorpion), in his right sleeve, and on the fingers of his left hand he fixed a 'wagnuk', or tiger's claws, a small steel instrument made to fit on the fore and little finger; it has three crooked blades, which are easily concealed in a half-closed hand.

THE WÂGNUK WITH WHICH SIWAJEE SEIZED ÁFZOOL-KHÁN.

(From "*Indian and Oriental Arms*," etc. By the Right Honourable Lord Egerton of Tatton.)

"Thus accoutred, he slowly descended from the fort. The Khán had arrived at the place of meeting before him, and was expressing his impatience at the delay, when Siwajee was seen advancing, apparently unarmed, and, like the Khán, attended by only one armed follower, his tried friend, Tánnájee Máloosray. Siwajee, in view of Áfzool Khán, frequently stopped, which was represented as the effects of alarm, a supposition more likely to be admitted from his diminutive size. Under pretence of assuring Siwajee, the armed attendant, by the contrivance of the Bráhmin Envoy, stood at a few paces' distance. Áfzool Khán made no objection to Siwajee's follower, although he carried two swords in his waistband, a circumstance which might pass unnoticed, being common amongst Mahrattas; he advanced two or three paces to meet Siwajee; they were introduced, and in the midst of the customary embrace, the treacherous Mahratta struck the wâgnuk into the bowels of Áfzool Khán, who quickly disengaged himself, clapped his hand on his sword, exclaiming 'Treachery and murder!'; but Siwajee instantly followed up the blow with his dagger. * The Khán had drawn his sword, and made a cut at Siwajee, but the concealed armour was proof against the blow. The whole was the work of a moment, and Siwajee was wresting the weapon from the hand of his victim before their attendants could run towards them. Syud Bundoo, the follower of the Khan, whose name deserves to be recorded, refused his life on condition of surrender, and against two such swordsmen as Siwajee and his companion, maintained an unequal combat for some time before he fell. The bearers had lifted the Khán into his palanquin during the scuffle, but by the time it was over Khundoo Málley and some other followers of Siwajee had come up, when they cut off the head of the dying man, and carried it to Pertabghur. The signals agreed on were now made; the Máwulees rushed from their concealment and beset the nearest part of the Beejapoor troops on all sides, few of whom had time to mount their horses or stand to their arms. Nettajee Pálkur with the Máwulees gave no quarter; but orders were

* *Vide* Frontispiece.

sent to Môro Punt to spare all who submitted; and Siwajee's humanity to his prisoners was conspicuous on this as well as on most occasions."

This graphic description is now shewn on very excellent authority to be not quite accurate—not quite fair to Siwajee. Mr. R. P. Karkharia, a Parsee historian of high repute, has hunted out old "bakhárs" (documents) of undoubted authenticity, and proves, in an able pamphlet on Pertabghur (or as he calls it Pratapgurh), that Áfzool Khán was only deceived so far as to believe that Siwajee was really in dread of him, that he came to the conference prepared not only to encounter treachery, but to employ it himself if opportunity offered. Áfzool Khán meant to surprise and seize, doubtless to kill, Siwajee, if the latter had not killed him, but he foolishly despised his enemy. Whatever treachery there was on both sides, was suggested by Bráhmins, prepared by Bráhmins—that much is certain!

The incident reads like one of the chapters in Fennimore Cooper's Red Indian Novels—we seem to see an encounter between the Crow Chief "Clawing Catamount" (Siwajee) and the Delaware leader "Big Bull" (Áfzool Khán), and we admire Siwajee's pluck, cunning, and superior military skill.

The mode of warfare, the morals of those years gone by are not to be judged by Exeter Hall standards of the present day. We have been dealing with times when armed and desperate men struggled daily to take each other's lives and snuffled not about murder. We may well cry, and let Mahrattas still cry, "Jèy! Siwajee Máháráj!" *—for he *was* a fine fellow; but when a handful of the treacherous caste that nullified his patriotism, suggested all his crimes, and compassed the downfall of the Empire he had raised, use his name for the furtherance of seditious plots against ourselves, 'tis surely the time to scotch the reptiles, not to subscribe to their schemes?

* Hurrah! (or victory) for Siwájee Máháráj

# CHAPTER VIII.

## THE INHABITANTS OF POONA.

### The Deccanee and Deccanised-Kônkanee Bráhmin.

JUST as it is unfair and unjust to condemn the entire Native Press because there are some seditious Vernacular and Anglo-Vernacular newspapers, so it is cruel and thoughtless to inveigh against all Bráhmins because there are some Bráhmin malignants. A caste that has produced the noble family of Vinchoor, the late Rao Sahèb V. N. Mandlik, the Hon. Justice Ránádè, the Barwès, the Atlàys, Messrs. S. H. Chiploonkur, and K. N. Bhángaokur, has many claims on our regard, and must have much good in it.

Let us take the case of the Vinchoorkur who has independent civil and criminal jurisdiction in some hundreds of villages in the Nassick District.

The Chief, disgusted with the treachery and cowardice of Bájee Rao, yet faithful to the very last, cast in his lot with the British after the Peishwa's abdication in 1818, and was of great service to Mr. Mountstuart Elphinstone in the pacification of the Deccan. Mr. Elphinstone confirmed him in his Jâgheer (Chieftainship) and gave him jurisdiction over all his towns and villages except the walled town of Yeola. This place, too, he promised should be restored to him when the country should be settled down. The Vinchoorkur family have consistently administered their Jâgheer with prudence, intelligence and uprightness, and have furnished several

THE DECCAN BRÁHMIN.

excellent servants to the British Government. No Chiefs have deserved so well at our hands, none have been so ill rewarded. It is not yet too late to restore Yeola to them, and it will be a disgrace if it be not restored. Had

Yeola been under Vinchoor it would, I am very sure, have maintained its high character, and there would have been no riots or disaffection there as of late.

Thus we snub, sit upon, humiliate, and deceive the loyal and influential classes, while we pet, pamper, and "kow tow" to the reptile Vernacular Press, owned and edited by nameless upstarts, whom we have seemingly educated for the purpose! We see the result now in Poona! Such is the outcome in India of the "policy of scuttle," which gave India Lord Ripon, which has ofttimes sent poor Bombay inexperienced, ignorant, and weak Pro-consuls because Party supporters must be provided for at any hazard: *which will lose India for us if it can.*

Could there be named a better specimen of the Deccanised Chitpâwan or Kônkanee Bráhmin than the late Rao Sahèb V. N. Mandlik, the friend of Sir Bartle Frere, Sir Barrow Ellis and many other distinguished Anglo-Indians?

What of the Honourable Justice Ránádè, a Deccanized-Kônkani Bráhmin? He has won his way up to the topmost rung of the ladder by sheer merit and ability; of unblemished character and integrity—a very Sagamore among his caste fellows—he has saved many a young man from egregious folly, has repressed judiciously and systematically the dangerous aspirations of pseudo-patriots by whom he has been surrounded all his life. These gentry, after the manner of such scum, now dare to revile and taunt him. His speech at the Jubilee meeting of the Elphinstone College is such a model of good taste, wisdom and good feeling that I cannot resist reproducing it here.

The Hon. Mr. Justice M. C. Ránádè said: "Mr. Principal and Professors, Ladies and Fellow-students, the only claim I have to speak at this gathering on behalf of the students both old and new, is that I am perhaps the oldest Elphinstonian present here to-day, having joined the College nearly 40 years ago. If not the oldest, I can certainly claim to be one who stayed longest within these walls; for, as student and as teacher, I was associated with the College for nearly fourteen years with one slight interruption. There are times, ladies and gentlemen, when our hearts are too full to permit of our giving adequate expression to the feelings which move us. This is just one of those occasions when all over the world, and notably in this country, in all our towns and villages, as well as in these busy Presidency centres, there is one central dominating idea exciting the imagination of millions in a way that cannot be easily compared to any similar event in our past history. Of course our past history furnishes a parallel of Sovereigns ruling over vast territories for more than half a century, and ruling over many millions of subjects with beneficence and wisdom. But nowhere except in the remotest part of mythical story, was there a commemoration so unique and universal as that which we witness before our eyes, not merely in the British Isles, but in all the great Colonies and dependencies in the four great continents, which own allegiance to the rule of our Empress-Queen. As students of history we should try to understand what lies at the root of all these wonderful manifestations of the devotion of millions and millions of men of all creeds and races to a ruler whom they perchance have never seen and will never see. Mere length of life cannot explain these phenomena, for, after all, long life is an accidental advantage which it is not given to man to command. The possession of power and of a world-wide empire by itself, whatever fear it might inspire, can never succeed in winning the hearts of millions over whom that power is exercised. There is something deeper than these possessions and accidents, which at the present time has thrown a spell over all of us, brought us together here to commemorate the sixtieth anniversary of Her Majesty's reign. There is a moral element at the base of all this display of force, and it is the triumph of this moral principle which alone has the power to move the hearts of millions in one unison of loyal and grateful sentiment. The Queen-Empress typifies in her person the ascendency of the reign of law in all departments of State activity. Herself a woman, she sits enthroned as the responsible head of the mightiest empire the world has yet known, and her personal character has enabled her to realise her responsibility as a constitutional ruler in a way which no mere paper constitutions, however skilfully framed, can ever secure. Some of you might think that, after all, law is but the expression of the Sovereign's will, which differentiates it in degree or kind from other expressions of her will, which we distinguish as orders and rules meant for executive convenience. To those who feel this difficulty I would suggest that they should turn their eyes inside into the recesses of their own hearts and see, if they can, if there is any law which is enthroned in their own hearts with authority, if not power, to rule over their own multifarious nature, passions, appetites, loves, hatreds. Their weakness is greatest when they yield obedience to these lower powers and disown the command of the law imprinted on their hearts.

"Their strength is irresistible when they regulate and subordinate their faculties and possessions to the rule of the Sovereign law enthroned in their hearts. The difference between man and man is a difference between obedience and disobedience to this law.

"What is true of the individual is if possible still more true in the case of collective bodies of men known as nations and empires. The British nation has its own faults and foibles, but there can be no question that in spite of these faults and foibles, their national character has been formed by ages of struggle and self-discipline in a world which illustrates better than any other contemporary power, the supremacy of what I have characterised as the reign of law. Just as in the individual the will when counselled and perfected by discipline and struggle, becomes the law for the man who listens to it, so in the collective nation it is when the Sovereign's will is similarly counselled and perfected by the advice of the estates and the free expression of public opinion, it becomes the dominant power in the land, to which every other subordinate power has to yield obedience, and which it has to carry out ungrudgingly. This is the secret of the moral force which sanctifies the sway of Britain over one-fifth of the globe and its entire population. In the absence of such a discipline mere power and fortune has a tendency to make men feel giddy, till oftentimes their very greatness helps to precipitate them into ruin. It is this moral principle which is the source of British greatness, and its armour and protection. It is also this same moral element which inspires hope and confidence in the colonies and dependencies of Great Britain, that whatever temporary perturbations may cloud the judgment, the reign of law will assert itself in the end. The long reign of Her Majesty has tended to strengthen the hold of this principle on the national mind, and her great personal ascendency is never so keenly appreciated as when she announces her determination to hold fast to this source of strength and to sympathise with the weakness, sorrows and sufferings of all her subjects. There have been in our own country good and beneficent Sovereigns, but their good and beneficent work has died with them. It is otherwise where impersonal law presides and rules over the destinies of men. There are of course ebbs and tides and temporary disturbances and even storms, but these only serve to bring into greater relief the calm majesty of the law overriding power and possession, more especially when this law is administered by the womanly instincts of one who has known sorrow and affliction herself. This is the moral secret of the charm which has endeared her home to millions and millions who have never seen her. This is why all the colonies and dependencies join with the British Isles in this commemoration, and this is the lesson which, on an occasion like this, I would ask the students of this college to take with them as the memory of an event which cannot fail

BRÁHMIN LADY.

to be remembered as a red-letter day on our country's annals. On behalf of the students I have great pleasure in thanking the Principal and Professors of the College for their kindness in inviting us all to take part in this commemorative gathering, and I hope such occasions will be far more frequent than they have hitherto been." (Loud cheers).

There are Bráhmins and Bráhmins. Methinks that the hot winds of the Deccan are deleterious to Bráhminical morals. Certainly the Chitpâwan in the Kônkan is usually a good man all round; as certainly the Deccan Bráhmin, with rare exceptions, like the chief of Vinchoor, is inferior to all of the caste. Certainly the Kônkanee Chitpâwan deteriorates morally when he settles above the Ghauts. The process can be watched in many a Chitpâwan family, part settled in Poona, part resident in the narrow strip of beautiful country won by Indra's prowess from Samudra (Neptune) at their duel at Hèlwak on the Koombarlee Ghâut. The legend is that when Indra came back with Luxmon a few billions of years afterwards to inspect his conquest, the latter insolently threw off his allegiance directly the pair stepped down on the red laterite soil of the Kônkan—that Indra (Máhá, or the great Indra) thereupon by a simple test * proved to Luxmon that his traitorous fit was due to the treacherous soil—that thereupon Luxmon pettishly exclaimed "Jalo!" ("May it burn!"), but that Máhá-Indra, with his usual magnanimity, qualified the curse—"Jalo pun peeko" ("May it burn, but produce"). The fable, as time has proved, is clearly a libel on the Kônkan and all Kônkanees, whether Bráhmins, Mahrattas or Mahommedans. But while change of climate does not demoralise either the second or third race (as

* By making Luxmon walk over a few yards of a path sprinkled with laterite soil.

witness the thousands of Kônkanee Mahrattas in mills and factories, on railways, in public and private service—as witness Kônkanee Mahommedans in highest places of trust and power, on the Bench, in Baroda and elsewhere), it does in a curious way demoralise the Kônkanee Bráhmin. Like the sap of the India-rubber tree when vulcanised, in moderately moist air it is supple, elastic, very useful, and fairly reliable. Expose it for any time, however, to the dry blasts of the Deccan and it loses tone, becomes brittle and unreliable—"Dekkan háwáchee goon ahe" ["It is the effect (or influence) of the Deccan climate!"]; Bájee Rao, Náná Sahèb, Tántia Topee, were all Kônkanee Bráhmins. It is quite conceivable that if they had lived out their lives at Sangamèshwar, or wherenot below the Ghauts, they might have shone in history as humane, benevolent administrators, but unfortunately their forbears would go to Poona and the Deccan, so their progeny developed into traitors and murderers!

There is something in the air of Poona, too, which produces that (to beholders) distressing disease, called "swelled-head" in America, just as the climate of the Straits brings on "elephantiasis" and "beri-beri." Young Bráhmins are very subject to it. Take a modest Chitpâwan youth from Chiploon, locate him at the Deccan College, and almost to a dead certainty, he will, in a few months become bumptious and overbearing. Young Deccan Bráhmins are almost all so afflicted—"Dekkan háwáchee goon ahe"—there is the solution in a nutshell!

The complaint is very difficult to eradicate in the Chitpâwan—it may be said to be incurable in the "Karrádee" or "Dèshast." The treatment found most efficacious is a strong infusion of ridicule, exhibited in large doses, as publicly as possible, and as often as one can catch the patient. This medicine has a marvellous effect on all Orientals, but somehow it operates immediately on Bráhmin cases, seems to reduce the swelling and to purify the blood, just as mouldy "soopari" (betel) nut clears any dog of worms! All Anglo-Indian officials should keep a few bottles on their office desks.

The Government of India have another remedy in their pharmacopœia, if they would but use it. It acts like caustic and burns up proud flesh, thus allaying surrounding inflammation. It is a compound of bitter contempt and icy language —no butter or oleaginous substance must be mixed with it. Viceroys and Proconsuls, though they should not ignore the National Congress and Congress-wallas, should not encourage the movement. Rather should they show by cool contempt that they disapprove. Congress-wallas should be struck off Government-House lists, systematically kept out in the cold, and, no matter how they may otherwise be distinguished, should not be patted on the back, anointed in Government Resolutions, or buttered up in speeches, still less should they be made Honourables in the Legislative Council.

One other Bráhmin point, and we will drop the sacred thread for the present. A hot-tempered, passionate Bráhmin, be he Deccanee or Kônkanee, is a rare bird—a prize fowl. When you find one, stick to him—he will stick to you—he is always a good fellow, usually a sharp and reliable servant. *Verb. sat. sap.*

# CHAPTER IX.

## INHABITANTS OF POONA.—*Continued.*

The pure Kônkanee Bráhmins. A Chitpâwan Legend.

THE principal Kônkanee Brahmins are (1) the Kônkanasthas commonly called the Chitpâwans, (2) the Deorookhas, (3) the Jáwalas. * For convenience' sake we will dispose of the two last first.

The Deorookhas take their name from a beautiful village and subdivision of that name in the Ratnagiri district; they abound in and about the old trading port, Rájápoor. The Peishwas encouraged them to settle further north, in Kolába and Tánnah, some of them even went as far as Baroda. They do not seem to have done much in Poona or the Deccan. Dr. Wilson mentions that they are considered unlucky, and that Chitpâwans, therefore, are shy of sitting in the same line with them. They are not well-to-do; though they are good farmers, they are, in the writer's experience, harsh landlords.

The Jáwalas' claim to be Bráhmins is not generally

* I purposely omit the Lingayet Bráhmins whose stronghold is in the Carnatic. Those in Poona are mostly in Government service. They are great rivals of the pure Bráhmins. They are more courageous, somewhat more reliable, but even more vindictive.

recognised by Chitpâwans, who allege that they were originally "koonbees" or cultivators, and that Purèshram Bhow Putwurdhan, the Peishwa's powerful relative, "made them Bráhmins for his own convenience." They used to eat fish, but are giving up the practice. They are especially numerous around Hurnee or Severndroog, where they hold some of the fattest rice lands. They have always been numerous in and near Poona, but have rarely occupied any exalted position.

The Chitpâwans are probably the fairest race in Hindoostan, often with blue or green-grey eyes; small, delicately formed hands and feet; well-cut, intellectual features; and generally a look of breeding that distinguishes them in any company. They have always been notable for intelligence and administrative ability, and number more men of mark in their history than all other castes put together; but they are innately cruel—they were the last and most bigotted supporters of "Suttee" (widow-burning). They are vindictive, treacherous, intriguing and untruthful, but mild, pleasing (or, rather, plausible) and courteous in manners. They are still, it is to be feared, as Messrs. Mountstuart Elphinstone and Chaplin recorded in 1818, "generally discontented, and only restrained by fear from being treasonable and treacherous." Their best men are passionate, like Rájá Sir Dinkur Rao—their worst are smooth and plausible, like Bájee Rao, the last Peishwa, and Náná Sahèb.

Most Anglo-Indians, however long they may have studied

their Chitpâwans will agree with the great missionary Rhenius, (Memoir, p. 187) that "nothing is so difficult to be understood and fully comprehended as a (Chitpâwan) Bráhmin's mind."

THE KÔNKANASTHA OR CHITPÂWAN BRÁHMIN
IN HIS KÔNKAN HOME.

Chitpâwans pretend to a superiority over other Bráhmins in descent as in physique and intellect, but they cannot justify their claim. They contend that "Chitpâwan" is synonymous with "Chitpôhle", which literally means "searing of the heart," and that they thus spoke of themselves as "heart-seared" or "heart-stricken", because the god Purèshram (Indra) did not grant all their prayers. The expression was not thought respectful by the god, so they changed it to "chitpâwan" or "pure-hearted," or "sinners pardoned". Their head-quarters, now called Chiploon, was originally Chitpôhlna. Other Bráhmins, and indeed Mahrattas generally, believe in a much less exalted tradition about them. Chitpâwan also means "a dead body raised." The legend is interesting. The author had the good fortune, nearly forty years ago, to make the acquaintance of an old "Bhutt" or Bráhmin bard at Chiploon: the old gentleman produced with some reluctance three Sanscrit "pôthees" or pamphlets, which no doubt were fragments of a work called "The Syádree Kind", which the Chitpâwan Peishwas suppressed or destroyed when they could get hold of them. * The first of these pamphlets related to the conquest of the Kônkan from the sea by Vishnoo (in his incarnation as Indra or Purèshram), which is briefly referred to at page 121 of this work. The second described the origin of the Chitpâwans and their immortality: the third showed how they doubted and treacherously deceived their god, and how Purèshram punished and made them mortal.

The author of this work does not profess to be a Pundit, nor is he writing for a Pundit public, he therefore reproduces the legend in a popular form, premising that he

* About 1814 Bájee Rao ruined and disgraced a respectable Dèshast Bráhmin of Waiee found in possession of a copy of "The Syádree Kind."

writes from memory, but that he had the books read and expounded to him by the aged bard aforesaid.

When Bráhma, the Supreme Being, had finished off creation by creating man, assuming human form he descended into the world as Vishnoo, also called Indra or Purèshram. For countless ages he waged war against the "Kshètriyas" or Hindoo Titans; it was a heavy undertaking. Twenty-five times did he believe that he had utterly destroyed them: twenty-five times did they reappear smiling: at the twenty-sixth engagement, however, he utterly exterminated them. Then he gave their territory, all Asia, to the Bráhmins, but they were ungrateful and refused to let him abide among them. The disgusted Indra then hied him with Luxmon to the edge of the Syádree mountains, to Hèlwák, just above Chiploon. "Samudra," the Hindu Neptune, then washed the summits of the range—witness marine shells in the face of the cliffs below the hill-fort of Wássôta. Indra insolently ordered the Ocean to retreat and give him territory to live in. Samudra refused. A duel *à l'outrance* was arranged, and Neptune, knowing and fearing Indra's powers with his bow, employed the interval in bribing the carpenter bee to bore through the centre of the weapon, so that when Indra, fitting his arrow, drew the bow it broke. So great, however, was Indra's strength that the arrow nevertheless flew out and dropped 18 koss (36 miles) into the Ocean's bosom, and Samudra acknowledging himself defeated, retreated that far.

Fairly content with his victory, Indra left his new kingdom to dry up, while he swaggered off on some other murderous business in Southern India. Returning with his brother and disciple Luxmon a few ages after, he sat him down at Hèlwák, (as described at page 121), descending to Chiploon, he beheld the country that it was exceeding fair to look upon, it only wanted peopling. This small matter was easily arranged. Neptune in derision cast up on the sands 14 dead bodies, probably of Arabs, which Indra promptly resuscitating, installed at Chiploon as Bráhmins, instructing them to build a shrine to him on a neighbouring hill, since called "Máindra" (Máhá Indra) or Purèshram. "I shall come there when I want rest," the god said, "and my spirit will always be there to protect you; meantime I give you these 'Sát Mullas, Sát Tullas,' (seven fat valleys, and seven tanks) wherefrom to irrigate them. Increase and multiply! Worship me and prosper! You shall never die like those Deccan rascals! Rám! Rám! Keep kind!"

So the god "took his hook" as the Baboos gracefully say, and left the immortal "twice-born" to their own devices.

For centuries the Chitpâwans did increase and multiply, for, sure enough, they never died. Becoming prosperous, they waxed bumptious, as Bráhmins are apt to do, and became a nuisance to mankind. The birds brought Indra intelligence of their oppressions and licentiousness. He saw he had made a great mistake, and, to rectify it, he bethought himself of instilling some of the "goon" or spirit of the red soil into the Chitpâwan mind. Accordingly, at the next meeting of the Bráhmin Elders under a certain wide-spreading Banian tree, when the conversation turned on their wondrous prosperity and immunity from death, he put it into the heart—or stomach (which is synonymous)—of an old gentleman to observe, "'Tis all very well, my brethren! True that none of us have yet died like those Dèshast Bráhmins above Ghâuts, or these impure Shudras (working men) round about us," (Here he spat vigorously on the ground.) "but what security have we after all that we never shall die, eh?" Animated discussion followed, in the course of which it was determined to test the god's good faith in this way: One of the party should sham dead, they would carry him up to the temple on the hill, and there extort some guarantee from the deity. No sooner said than done: the counterfeit corpse, decently laid out on a bier, his face besmeared with ochre and red pigment, was carried toilsomely up to the shrine, escorted by a posse of caste mourners, naked to the waist, "oogada bôdka" (bareheaded), swinging pots of burning incense, and making the welkin ring with their wail "Arè Nárráyen! Nárráyen!" Depositing the burthen before the idol and ringing the bell overhead to attract the god's attention, an old grey-beard took up the parable "Arè, Deoba (" Look here, old god), you promised we should never die, but see what we have brought you!" (Pointing to the shammer.) "What security will you give us that death shall not again visit us?" A solemn silence followed, broken only by the muttered "muntrees" (imprecations) of the Poojárree (priest) as he walked round and round the altar, ever and anon dropping flowers on the idol and sprinkling it with holy water. Lo! the blossoms drop with-

Máhindra or Purèshram. THE STRONGHOLD OF THE CHITPÁWAN BRÁHMINS. Helwàk.
Gowalkote Fort at head of River Wáshistee. Chiploon.
*(See page 129.)*

ered—will not rest on the idol! The water evaporates in steam! Horror of horrors! The priest faints, and pitchy darkness fills the shrine-room! Suddenly a terrific flash of lightning reveals the deity to the terror-stricken conspirators, and a voice thunders, "Treacherous and accursed race! the cup of your iniquities is filled to overflowing (ápalè pâp bharilè gèle)! Ye ask a sign! Take it from that bier! So shall ye all die in future!" Behold the shammer was as dead as any Dèshast!

"The story is quite true, Sahèb," said the old bard. "*There* is the Banian tree out there by the tank; *there* are the seven 'Mullas' and 'Tullas,' still so registered in the Revenue Register of the town, and Chitpáwan Bráhmins die—Vishnoo be praised!—like other people."

# CHAPTER X.

## THE INHABITANTS OF POONA.—*Continued.*

### The Sárasawata, Senoy, or Shènwee Bráhmins.

THIS important caste of the Panch-Gauda Bráhmins take their name from the Sáraswatee river (shewn as the Cagger in old maps) which, belonging to the North-Western system of rivers rising in the Siwalik range, flows past Thànesur and loses itself in the sands "on its approach to the (non-Aryan) Nishádas." (Vol. 1, p. 251, of the "Máhábhárata".) They are found in the Punjaub, Sinde, Rájpootana, Guzerát and the Kônkans above Goa. According to the learned Doctor Bhow Dájee—who was a Shènwee—they have only been settled in the Kônkans for about 700 years. "Shènwee," according to the Reverend Dr. Wilson, is probably a malicious nick-name given by the Chitpâwan Bráhmins, who affirm that they are descended from a lascivious Chitpâwan, who finding a low-caste girl gathering "Shèn" or cow-dung, made her a mother. The other derivation suggested by the reverend gentleman seems much more probable—viz., that Shènwee is an abbreviation of a Kanarese word, "Shànbog," which means a scribe or village accountant.

From time immemorial Shènwees have been distinguished

at the desk, on the field of battle, in diplomacy and government, in commerce, and latterly in literature and science, especially medicine and surgery. The Sindias' ministries were almost entirely composed of Shènwees, who proved always staunch and reliable in a crisis, sagacious

A SHÈNWEE STUDENT.

in council, courageous in action. Bálloba Tattya, many times referred to in my historical sketch, was a typical Shènwee of his times. During the present century, despite the jealousy and virulent opposition of the Bráhmins, they have steadily risen in all branches of public life; for they are not vindictive, they ar enot over-bearing, nor cruel when in power, they are not rapacious nor miserly, but generous and fair in their dealings, and they are the best of friends. It has been the fashion to say that they are not so astute as the Bráhmins. They may not be so quick and, in so far as astuteness means cunning, they are certainly incapable of those intricate intrigues which are the very life of many of the cleverest Bráhmins. They may not be so quick at discerning character, but their judgment is sounder and more charitable. They are known to fame on the Judicial Bench (witness Justice Telang)—they are sound lawyers (witness Shantaram Nárráyen)—they are eminent educationists (witness Professor Bhándarkar). They are shrewd and enterprising merchants (witness Rugonath Nárráyen Khote and Nárráyen Wâsoodeo Dâbholekar). The list of scientific men is full of Shènwee names (witness Drs. Bhow and Nárráyen Dáji, Dádoba and Átmáram Pándoorung). They are imbued with true public spirit and have furnished some of Bombay's best citizens. In short, they are a class of which any country might well be proud. In the Shènwees the Government will always find the best antidote to Bráhminical poison, for they are perhaps the most loyal and reliable of all Hindoos.

There are many, but not enough of them in State employ.

# CHAPTER XI.

## THE INHABITANTS OF POONA.—*Continued.*

### The Parbhu—Prabhu—(Anglice) Purvoe.

ACCORDING to Bráhminical views the Parbhu or Prabhu ranks lower than the Shudra (working-man) in the scheme of mixed castes: he may be a Káyastha, descended from a Vaidehikar (or Vaidy) father and a Máhishya or Jôshi mother —or from a Káyastha father and a Káyastha widow—or from a Vratiya Prabhu brother and a Prabhu sister by incestuous intercourse, as vilely insinuated by Bráhmin writers, Káyasthas or Parbhus being from the early days of Máháráshtra down nearly to the present day "great rivals in the matter of office employment" (*Vide* Dr. Wilson, "*Indian Caste*", Vol. 1, page 66).

They entered the British service in great numbers from the very beginning of the rise of our power, as clerks, secretaries, and confidential agents, so that, in the military departments especially, they occupied all the office stools, and office clerks were generally called Purvoes.

They still fill most military posts, but in Civil departments, even in the Secretariat where they have deservedly occupied positions of great trust, they are gradually being ousted by Bráhmins, not by any means to the advantage of the State.

They are a peculiarly inoffensive, quiet, well-conducted caste, with a high reputation for fidelity and integrity. They are very tender in their treatment of their women,

THE PARBHU.

who are rarely permitted to soil themselves in domestic drudgery. Many Prabhu ladies were highly educated ere ever female education found favour with the Bráhmins. They seem to have gradually lost energy during the last fifty years, and their decadence is much to be deplored.

That they are innately courageous and were possessed of no little military skill, is proved by Mahratta history.

When Siwajee, in 1655, stormed the Fort of Rohira, Bájee Parbhu Dèshpándye, of Hurdás Máwul, headed the defenders with such gallantry that Siwajee, out of admiration, not only confirmed him in all his hereditary offices and possessions, but taking him into his service, placed him in command of a large body of his Hèdkaree and Máwulee infantry. Well did Bájee requite this confidence! In September 1660, when Siwajee, finding himself shut up by Fazil Khán and the Seedees Johur and Uzeez in Panálla, escaped and was pursued to Rángna, he placed Bájee Parbhu with a body of Máwulees in a pass six miles from the fort, with orders to hold it at any cost until he heard the signal of five guns, which should announce that Siwajee with the main body of his followers were safe in Rángna. Bájee first drove back the cavalry with great slaughter, two assaults by fresh infantry were similarly repulsed, but about midday the son of Áfzool Khán headed a third desperate attack with overwhelming numbers, when Bájee, having lost half his little band, retreated, after hearing the signal given from Rángna. He was killed immediately afterwards and died expressing his satisfaction. "The Máwulees proved their regard for him, as well as their own steadiness, by bearing off his body in the face of their numerous pursuers." There is no more stirring incident in Siwajee's wonderful career.

Another Bájee Parbhu Dèshpandye, of Mhár,—no relation, however—in the same year heroically defended

Poorandhar for a long time against Dilère Khán, the Môgul general, and repulsed his Pathans and Afghans, "when Dilère Khán, having marked the conspicuous conduct of their leader, with his own hand pierced him with an arrow and killed him on the spot" (Grant Duff, vol. 1, pages 174, 176).

Bállajee Aujee Chitnees also was a Prabhu so highly esteemed by Siwajee that he offered to make him one of his Council of Purdhans. Bállajee, probably foreseeing that he would soon fall a victim to Bráhmin intrigue, refused the honour. He remained staunch to Sôyera Bye, Siwajee's widow, after Siwajee's death, and when this lady was murdered by Sumbhajee (see page 106) he, his son Sámjee, Annajee Dutto, and many of the Shirkay family strove their utmost to support Rájá Ram, her son, and to avenge her death. Sumbhajee discovering their intrigues, trapped them all at Panálla (in 1681), and caused them to be trampled under the feet of elephants.

It was a Prabhu again who defended the Fort of Sátára against Aurungzebe himself in 1699. Práyágjee Parbhu, who had risen to note under Siwajee, commanded the gallant garrison, who rolled down huge stones, which "were as destructive as artillery" (Grant Duff, pages 334 to 336). In 1700 the Môguls exploded several mines at the foot of the scarp, one of which exploding outwards, destroyed 2,000 of the besiegers. Another exploded inwards and Práyágjee Parbhu was buried in the ruins, close to a temple of Bhowánee, but, to the delight of the garrison, was dug out alive. Starved out, he capitulated at last with all the honours of war. I have been unable to trace Práyágjee further.

These are only a few illustrations from ancient history of the courage and fidelity of Parbhus. There are many others in our own rule in Western India. There are few Parbhus in Poona City besides the employés in Government offices. They have not much influence there, but what little they possess is certainly exercised for good.

## CHAPTER XII.

### THE MAHRATTAS OF THE SYÂDREES, OF THE GHAUT MÁHTA, OF THE PLAINS.

In a future chapter I shall deal with the pure type of Kônkanee Mahommedan to be found settled as small farmers and land-owners near the foot of the Syadree Range, mostly between the Savitree and Wáshistee rivers. Even more interesting are the few Mahratta families in their immediate neighbourhood, who are to be found still further eastward, in villages and hamlets perched on the great spurs running down from the Ghauts, or nestling in the stupendous ravines that penetrate to the very foot of the range, from Mhyputghur, near Máhábalèshwur, as far as the Phônda Ghaut, one hundred and twenty miles southward, where they come in contact with the Sáwants and other Mahratta families of inferior descent who have spread upwards from Sáwantwaree.

The Syadree type of Mahratta differs entirely from the ordinary Mahratta one is familiar with in the Deccan, and few specimens are to be met in or about Poona. They become more numerous, however, to the North and East of Khándeish, in Málwa, and in the Central Provinces, and branches of the leading families have long been settled in the

Gaekwár's, Sindia's and Hôlkar's dominions. Instead of being swarthy and short, they are nearly as fair-skinned as Bráhmins of the higher castes, and, for Hindoos, they are of lofty stature, well but sparely built, with regular and often very handsome features. They carry themselves

THE MAHRATTA OF THE SYÁDREES.

with great native dignity, and though habitually reserved and somewhat abrupt in manner, there is an indescribable air of refinement and high breeding in all they do or say. Their traditions are essentially warlike, and the surnames they bear, "Shirkè", "Mâlusray", "Mánkar", and the like, recall many a stirring incident in Mahratta history. Martial spirit exists as strong as ever it was amongst them, and will never die out; but for some reason or other they have generally been disinclined to take service in the British Army. Their young men early seek, and readily obtain, employment in the forces maintained by the principal Mahratta States, and the heads of the families resident along the Syadrees are military pensioners of, or draw some small allowance from, some native "Ráj" or other.

There are various theories as to their origin. Some authorities believe them to be descendants of leaders of Siwajee's "Hèdkarees", who were rewarded for services in the field by grants of lands and villages along the Ghauts—much as the Bráhmin hangers-on of the Peishwas subsequently received villages in "Khotee"; other authorities insist that they made their appearance on the Western Ghauts long after the rise of the Peishwas; they themselves, however, mostly claim to be of Rájpoot descent, and to have originally ruled as petty Rájahs and Chieftains down to the coast itself, retreating with their followers step by step eastward into the fastnesses of the Ghaut range, as trade, and then piracy, advanced from the seaboard.

To them, and the cultivators who followed them, is probably due the denuded condition of the Ghaut spurs, which has had such serious results, and is so justly and bitterly bewailed by enthusiasts of the Forest Department. We know that originally the western slopes of the whole length of this mountain range must have been clothed with dense jungle, often with large-tree forest, which has almost entirely disappeared. On the sheltered side of ravines tree vegetation certainly does still exist in places, but it consists only of small teak, "ain", and "kinjal" trees, annually lopped and pollarded to provide that "râb", * without which the miserable soil will produce no crops. The slopes, plateaux and undulations are as bare as the back of one's hand! The ancestors of the present inhabitants adopted a very simple expedient for clearing the ground; they fired the forest in the hot season: for every acre they wanted they burnt ten, fifteen or a hundred acres of good forest, and no doubt raised some plenteous crops of "náglee" and "waree" (coarse millet) while the virtues of the ash remained in the soil. When the soil was exhausted, they simply burned a little more forest and shifted their huts. Bands of "Oopree", or wandering cultivators, came up from the lowlands, engaged with the "Raos", or Mahratta village headmen, to stay two, three or four years on payment of an almost nominal grain rental, with the understanding that they should clear so much jungle while in the neighbourhood. As the cultivators moved on, abandoning the worn-out land behind them, it gradually became covered again with dense scrub, which in the course of a decade was again burnt. Thus the wasteful system of what is called "Kumree" cultivation went merrily on, and all large forest growth was destroyed. Exposed to a rainfall of three and four hundred inches, with no

* Brushwood and leaves which are spread over the seedbeds and then fired.

undergrowth to retain it, the soil has been carried away, and the silt has gone to enrich the valleys, or choked up the heads of large estuaries, leaving what were large trading ports, such as Chiploon, Sangamèshwur, Rájápur, and Khárèpátan, high and dry, or only accessible by vessels of very small draft.

It will be gathered from the above that there cannot be much prosperity along the Ghauts. In 1860 I was directed for a special purpose to visit as many of these mountain villages as I could during the cold weather, between Pôladpur and Chiploon. A fair view of the ground traversed can be seen from Bombay Point, at Máhábalèshwur, looking south over Mhyputghur, Sumárghur, and Ressálghur. As everything had to be carried in head loads, and the population is scanty, I travelled as lightly as possible, trusting to the heads of villages to run me up some temporary shelter from the sun and dew when there was no decent shed or verandah available. I crossed the spurs from village to village when I could, or when the hills were too precipitous I went round by the valleys. I had to live on milk, eggs, "chuppatis" * and the inevitable "sudden death", † or such doves and pigeons as I could shoot. It was hard work and a rough life, but I can truly say I never enjoyed a trip so much as this. So far as I could learn only two Europeans had then ever been in those parts before, and I was received with the utmost hospitality and

* Unleavened cakes.

† Chicken.

civility—*not* servility—in every village, and had great difficulty in inducing the "Rao" to accept payment for supplies.

In the good old days I wot of the "Raos" led a truly patriarchal life, rarely leaving their village to visit the towns in the lowlands. Their word was law to their Koonbee cultivators. Every local dispute was referred to and settled by them. Moneylenders or shopkeepers there were none in these Mahratta villages, and there was no need of them. The harvest yielded sufficient grain to pay the "Rao" his rent in kind, and to support the cultivators. Now and again a trader (usually a Mahommedan) found his way up the valley with a string of pack ponies or bullocks laden with salt, salt fish, coarse cloth, "kumblies" (blankets), oil, and the like, which he bartered away for grain, at the same time purchasing most of the "Rao's" grain stock for cash to enable him to pay his Government assessment. The "Raos" helped their ryots to get along from harvest to harvest, and if a bad year came they helped each other or starved together courageously. I remember reporting to Government during the great famine of 1877, that there were few years in which the denizens of these Ghát villages did not suffer privations that would be termed famine in the Deccan!

I found that in some of these villages, where there was more than one branch of a "Rao" family, they put their grain into a common stock, and lived almost together, most amicably. In others they had either divided the lands among themselves, or had divided the ryots; in hardly any case was there any dissension among the co-sharers. The Government revenue was recognised as the first liability, and it was, as a rule, paid with exemplary punctuality. The vice of drunkenness was unknown—indeed, there were no liquor shops. Such a thing as civil process was unheard of. There were no criminal classes, and property of every kind was safe. Occasionally, however, there was a boundary dispute between one village and another, when a free fight would occur, in which the "koiti" or bill-hook was sometimes used with fatal effect. Otherwise the people were peaceable and law-abiding in a remarkable degree. I remember only one dreadful tragedy, which I will relate.

It occurred in one of the largest villages I camped in; Dhámansee was, I think, its name. When I arrived the wedding of the eldest son of the senior "Rao" was being celebrated with much rejoicing. There were two "Raos", brothers, who owned the village, both old men who had in their youth served in Sindia's army. They lived together in the principal house in the village, and between them performed such duties as appertained to the office of police "karbharee" or patell. In those days, I may mention, the police patells (headmen) in the Kônkan received no remuneration whatever, and it was a matter of course for the head or heads of the village to hold the office. Rámájee Rao, the bridegroom, was a strapping young fellow of about four and twenty, already a naique at Gwalior, whence he had obtained long furlough to marry a girl of about fifteen years of age belonging to a neighbouring good family. His father and uncle were delighted at the match; the villagers kept high festival, and I was right glad to get away from the incessant din of the tom-toms and the bray of the "shingárás" (long curly horns). Shortly afterwards I was transferred to the southern part of the district, and having to come up to head-quarters to give evidence in a Sessions case, I learnt to my horror that young Rámájee Rao was to be tried for the murder of his wife!

It came about in this way. The newly married couple resided as a matter of course in the family dwelling at Dhámansee till the time came for him to rejoin his regiment at Gwalior. Naturally he wanted to take his wife with him, but her parents, on the other hand, wished her to return to them for a time. The girl herself wanted to go with Rámájee Rao, but was over-persuaded by her mother, and refused. Rámájee Rao became incensed, and on one or two occasions chastised her somewhat brutally. His father and uncle—who had till then taken his part, then turned against him, and at almost the last moment it was decided in family conclave that the girl should return with her parents to her own village on the following morning, and that Rámájee Rao should return alone to Gwalior. Rámájee Rao seemingly was pacified. He and his wife retired as usual to sleep in an inner chamber, while the father and uncle rolled themselves up in the verandah. In the middle of the night the father was awakened by some curious noises in the inner room. Calling out and receiving no answer, he groped his way into the room, and felt himself kicked, as it were, in the face. His shouts brought in his brother and the household, with lights, when the almost lifeless body of Rámájee Rao was found suspended to a beam. He was promptly cut down, and with much difficulty resuscitated. His first ejaculations led the bystanders to look for his young wife, whose existence had been quite forgotten during the excitement. She was found in a corner of the room, stone dead, with protruding eyes and tongue, having evidently been strangled by Rámájee Rao before he hanged himself.

In nine such cases out of ten I venture to affirm that the first thoughts of the relatives would be to hush the matter up if possible. The brave old father and the uncle, however, never hesitated for a moment; they bound Rámájee Rao hand and foot; the old uncle called two Mhárs and set off then and there for a ten miles' trudge to report the occurrence at the nearest police post, while the old father sat him down and kept guard over his son till the police came and took charge of him!

I could not bring myself to hear the trial, but Mr. Claude Erskine, the Judge who tried it, and was deeply affected, afterwards told me that he never witnessed anything like the fortitude with which those two grand old fellows gave their evidence. A death sentence was passed of course, but the Sudder Court mercifully commuted it to transportation for life.

The incident will serve to show the kind of stuff of which these fine old Mahrattas are made. I much fear that what with Revenue Survey Settlements, Forest Demar-

SYÁDREE MAHRATTAS—FATHER AND SON.

cations, Civil Procedure Codes, Khotee and Ryots Protection Associations, to say nothing of vakils, liquor shops, and moneylenders, the Arcadian state, which I have attempted to depict has long since disappeared.

### THE MAHRATTAS OF THE GHAUT—MÁHTA AND THE MÁWULS—"GHÁTTEES".

These are undoubtedly the descendants of Siwajee's redoubtable Máwullees—of medium height, well-knit powerful frames, they are capable of incredible and sustained exertion. For many years they have thrown away the sword and devoted themselves to the more peaceful pursuits of civilisation. They worked splendidly in large gangs on the tunnels, rock cuttings, and viaducts on the Bhôre Ghaut Railway Incline. Thence they migrated almost in a body to Bombay to the reclamation and dock works. It was marvellous to see with what ease and skill they transported and placed *in situ* the huge granite blocks for the dock sills and gates. They are among the best labourers in the world. As they work hard they live well—generally in messes of ten or twenty—and devour vast quantities of mutton and fish. They drink hard of course, and their innate fierceness breaks out in their quarrels over their cups. Earning the highest wages of unskilled labour, they have no inclination to return to their mountain homes, where want would soon drive them to violent lives. Many of them have risen to be wealthy sub-contractors on public works—of these a few reside in Poona. All bear a character for integrity and fairness in their dealings. It has been a wonderful reclamation of a turbulent, high-spirited, absolutely fearless race, to the paths of peace, and respect for law and authority.

### THE MAHRATTAS OF THE PLAINS.

The typical Mahratta of the "Dèsh" or plains of the Deccan is the Patell or hereditary headman of his village—the large farmer and land-holder—a breeder of good horses—vying with his neighbours in rearing fine horned cattle. Centuries of misrule under governments constantly changing—centuries of oppression and anarchy—have not spoilt him or weakened his influence, which is usually exercised for good. No other country can show a peasantry so well controlled by hereditary village petty magistrates, and that at an almost nominal cost—in no other country are the government dues so easily or so punctually collected. This is all the work of the Muccadum or officiating police and revenue headmen, many of whom are now entrusted with extended magisterial powers, and exercise them at least as well as the majority of the unpaid magistracy in English rural districts. Education, it is true, has made slow progress among the "Dèsh" Mahrattas, but this has not been so much their fault as the result of Bráhmin efforts to prevent it. What progress has been made has at any rate been sound and healthy, and tended to the better administration of the country-side. Meantime many of the oldest families are represented, many have gained distinction, in the army, both horse and foot, and all are faithful to their salt.

## CHAPTER XIII.

### THE KÔNKANEE MUSSULMAN.

THE Kônkan Mahommedanee occasionally settles in the Deccan; he is to be found at Poona, but is to be seen at his best in a comparatively small region, to wit, the Khèd and Dapoolie Talukas, sub-districts of Ratnágiri. There will be found a few small clusters of villages, situate not only on the borders of the Jôgbarree and Wâshistee rivers, but lying well inland also, which, with the exception of just enough Mahratta cultivators to carry on farm labour, and a few Mhârs to act as watchmen, guides and messengers, are entirely peopled by Mahommedans, who at once impress the observer as worthy of special study. Their dress, to begin with, is remarkable, inasmuch as they surmount the usual Mahommedan jacket, shirt and pyjamas, with a large Bráhminical turban, casting a scarf or shawl round their necks, very much in the fashion of that worn by Bráhmins in gala dress. Somehow the costume, incongruous as it may appear from this description, goes exceedingly well with the grave demeanour, handsome features, and dignified bearing of the wearers. They are usually rather above the average height and always well built, with small, well-proportioned hands and feet; their profiles are clear cut, the nose generally aquiline; full frank eyes, and massive foreheads; the whole betokening their descent from the best Mahommedan blood in Northern India. Their presence as superior landowners in this out-of-the-way part of Western India, is very difficult to account for; but prob-

THE KÔNKANEE MUSSULMAN.

ably their ancestors received grants of their lands for services performed during the Môgul and Beejápur dynasties. Judging from the number of ruined mosques and "Peer's" (saint's) tombs scattered about, there must have been rather a large Mahommedan population in that neighbourhood at some time or other before the Peishwa's ráj. Large numbers of them, however, abandoned their lands and villages as they became surrounded by Bráhmin and Mahratta Khôtes. * A few of the wealthier of the best old families only remain now, and many of these are dying out or have been driven by adverse circumstances to seek a livelihood elsewhere. Mahommedans are invariably kind and liberal landlords, but they are shockingly bad farmers and cultivators, and their personal expenditure is lavish and extravagant compared with that of their Hindoo neighbours. As a natural consequence, they fall an easy prey to local usurers, who are the real owners of most of their villages now.

Great numbers of these Kônkanee Mahommedans flocked to the service of the British Government during the settlement of the Kônkan after the overthrow of the Peishwa: they were largely employed in the Customs Department, and many of the first Mamlutdars † and Máhálkarees were taken from the old Mahommedan families at and near Bankote and the Khèd subdistrict, where the Parkárs, Pôtricks, Sajánees and others were very influential and very deservedly respected. The chief revenue official in 1820 was a splendid old gentleman, the head of the Parkárs of Bankôte, who, despite his advanced age, insisted on leading the stormers at the capture of several forts by Colonel Prothero and other commanders. Several of his descendants rose to high official rank in various departments, and one of them was,

* Middlemen or Farmers of Revenue.

† Subdistrict Officers.

very many years ago, State Kârbharee § to the late Nawab of Jinjira. When I first went to Ratnágiri in 1859—60, Mr. Turquand's "chitnis" (secretary) was a Mahommedan: there were also two Mahommedan Mamlutdars and several Máhálkarees. Gradually the Bráhmins have shouldered them out of every post: impoverished and apathetic, their families have been indifferently educated, so that they have never qualified for Government service, except in the lower grades of the police. 'Tis a thousand pities! For the Kónkanee Mussalman is intelligent, resolute, faithful, and thoroughly to be depended upon in an emergency.

Somewhere about 1850 there was in the Revenue Department a very promising young Mahommedan gentleman, whom, for certain reasons, I will call Abdul Farreed. He belonged to one of the best of the old families I have alluded to above. He had entered the Revenue Department as a mere Kárkun or clerk, and forced his way upwards by dint of sheer ability and energy till he was made a Máhálkaree. At that time there was a great scarcity of food grains in the Kônkan, a scarcity such as in the present day would be called a famine, and Khán Sahèb Abdul Farreed greatly distinguished himself by the efforts he made to obtain food through his relatives and friends in Bombay, and to distribute supplies to the poor people of all creeds and castes in his jurisdiction; so much so, that he received on more than one occasion the thanks of the Government. It was a common thing then for parents reduced nearly to starvation to expose

§ Prime Minister.

their infants in spots where they would be soon discovered, in the hope that some charitable persons might find, take charge of, and rear them. In this way a little girl about eighteen months old was found at the roadside in Abdul Farreed's jurisdiction, and brought to him. He took the infant into his family, and his women folk cherished and brought her up. Fearful that his conduct might some day be misrepresented, he reported to his official superior what he had done, and that it was his intention to bring the child up as a member of his own family. He received in due course the commendations of Government for his charity. Time passed, and he was promoted to a "Mamlat" (subdistrict) at a distance. There he incurred the enmity of the Bráhmins, who lost no opportunity of trying to injure him in the eyes of the Collector and the Magistrate. Anonymous letters accusing him of every crime under the sun poured in. Conspiracies innumerable were got up against him, but Khán Sahèb Abdul Farreed, though he continued to triumph over his enemies, and retained the full confidence of his chief, became disheartened. His request to be transferred to some other district where he hoped to encounter less hostility, was refused. Abdul Farreed, who had some private means, thereupon tendered his resignation on the ground that he could not hope to prevail always against the secret machinations of his enemies. His chief refused to accept his resignation, and with much difficulty persuaded him to stay on and not give his detractors the satisfaction of having driven him away.

This chief not long afterwards left the District, and was succeeded by a gentleman who knew not Abdul. This was the opportunity his enemies desired. In a marvellously short time they concocted a diabolical conspiracy, with the aid of some of his own Mahratta peons. The body of a Bráhmin widow was found in a well, and Khán Sahèb Abdul Farreed was anonymously accused of having had her brought to his house by certain peons, and finally, after violating her, of having with the aid of other peons, caused her to be thrown into the well. He was suspended from office, committed to the Sessions, and after lying in jail for nearly six months, was arraigned for murder. He had not the means to engage an English barrister—in fact, there were very few in those days who would undertake a case out of Bombay. He would not trust any Bráhmin pleader, and there was no Mahommedan Vakil, so he defended himself. After a long and patient trial, in which he very ably exposed certain discrepancies in the evidence of the peons, he was acquitted. He would no doubt have been reinstated had he cared to petition, but he felt himself to be hopelessly disgraced, and preferred to retire to his native village, where he shut himself up and lived a life of complete seclusion with his family, rarely permitting even his brothers to visit him.

As a matter of fact Abdul Farreed had had no acquaintance whatever with the family of the deceased widow, whom he had never even seen; and circumstances afterwards came to light which proved beyond doubt that the unfortunate woman when drawing water from the well had accidentally overbalanced herself, fallen in, and been drowned. This collapse of the case against Abdul Farreed, so far from discouraging his enemies, emboldened them to enter upon a fresh system of persecution. Abdul Farreed was pursued into his retirement a hundred and fifty miles distant, by continuous accusations of corruption and malversation of public monies, in all of which, however, he came out triumphant. Then, for about two years, with the exception of scurrilous anonymous letters to himself and petitions to the magisterial authorities—none of which were ever traced to their source—Abdul Farreed was left in comparative peace. He built a wall round his property to secure privacy, and devoted himself to the observances of religion, and to horticulture, of which he was passionately fond. He also devoted much of his leisure time to preparing a series of notes on the subjugation of the Kônkan, which would have been of great value had they ever seen the light.

In the meantime the little waif, whom he had charitably taken into his family some years before, arrived at a marriageable age. She had been named "Khatiza", had been cherished and educated in his Zenáná, and taught to regard him as her father. It was known among the Mahommedan gentry throughout the country-side and in the neighbouring Mahommedan State of Habsán, that he was trying to obtain a suitable husband for her, and was prepared to give her a very handsome dowry, considering what his own means were. It would be difficult, one would have thought, to distort his admirable behaviour in regard to this poor child into a ground for accusing him of any fresh crime; but his enemies were as unscrupulous as they were remorseless. They had, of course, made themselves fully acquainted with his early history, in the hope of finding some vulnerable point on which they might attack him, and they knew of the incident of the discovery of the infant girl Khatiza, and of her having been adopted into Abdul Farreed's family.

So long as she was a child there was nothing that he could be accused of in regard to her; but it was different when she arrived at maturity. They could then—and in their diabolical hatred of him they did—make all kinds of infernal suggestions. Anonymous letters were constantly received by the authorities warning them that a fresh and terrible tragedy was impending at Abdul Farreed's house: that he had given way to drink; that he had evil designs on Khatiza; that she was only saved from his violence by the ladies of his own Zenáná, who shielded and protected her; that these ladies sought to place her with one of his elder brothers for safety, "lest there should be a repetition of his former crime," but that they could not break through the restrictions with which he had surrounded his prison-like house.

The Magistrate was besought to surround and search the house, to summon the ladies, and take their evidence, to release Khatiza at all hazards: the writers knowing that no greater indignity could be offered to a Mahommedan gentleman than the searching of his house, or the summoning of his womankind for any purpose. Needless to say that these anonymous communications were treated with contempt, though they were filed, and enquiries made in the hope of tracing the writers.

I myself received, month after month, documents of this kind, and having struck up a warm friendship with Abdul Farreed's eldest brother, consulted with him as to the best mode of terminating once and for ever this particular form of persecution. Mahomed Farreed was advanced in life, a man renowned for his blameless life; he had always shown the greatest sympathy for his younger brother, who, however, had repulsed all his advances. After many consultations it was agreed between us that there was but one way of checkmating Abdul Farreed's enemies, so far at least as the insinuations regarding Khatiza were concerned. Abdul must be persuaded to let her leave his house and be placed under Mahomed's protection till she was married, as it was hoped she soon would be. My friend Mahomed tried in vain to induce his younger brother to assent, telling him of the interest I took in the matter and my object; he showed Abdul also some of the vile letters I had received, but these only made him more obdurate. Finally, I resolved on making an attempt to see Abdul myself, and not long afterwards I visited the village of the Farreeds, told Mahomed what I was about to do, and myself went and asked to see Abdul at his own house. As may be imagined, there was much commotion when I knocked at the gateway: an ordinary visitor would have been treated very unceremoniously, but I sent in my name with a note from Mahomed, and simply asked to see Abdul for a few moments at the gateway, adding that I should not go away till I did see him.

After a considerable interval, the gate was opened by as fine a specimen of the Mahommedan race as it has ever been my good fortune to see. Nearly six feet high, and broad in proportion, erect in carriage, with a long beard that fell nearly to his waist, clear-cut but massive features, with intelligent eyes, and an expression in them of deep despair, yet of resignation: it was impossible to associate such a man with violence or depravity. A few hurried words passed between us: I apologising for my intrusion, and striving to excuse it—he, with the tears streaming down his face, trying to maintain a çalm appearance, while in broken words he said, "I never thought to see a Sahèb's face again." We seemed to take to each other at once. With all the grace and dignity which distinguish a well-born Mahommedan, he asked me into his house, into a handsomely furnished room, fitted as a library, where for nearly two hours we discussed his past history and most unfortunate position. I told him that his brother was the most intimate native friend I possessed—that I had made it my business to master all the details of the infamous conspiracy of which he had been a victim, in the hopes of being able by some means or other to reach the authors of it. I recounted to him the

FORT VICTORIA—BÁNKÔTE.
Mouth of the river Sávitree. Principal home of Kônkanee Mahommedans.

hideous case of Vinayek Deo, the "would-be parricide," which I have published separately, * and which I had just before disposed of. I impressed upon him the great importance, for the sake of his family, of his coming out again into the world and showing his enemies that they had not utterly broken him down; but it was all of no avail, so far as his own personal feeling was concerned. He persisted that he was a broken-hearted man, hopelessly disgraced in the eyes of the world, and all he desired was to be permitted to die in peace. I then gradually brought the conversation to the question of the girl Khatiza, told him what his enemies were insinuating about her and him, and suggested that the one way to stop these attacks, and, above all, to protect her fair fame, was to place her in his brother Mahomed's family and let her be thence married. He was deeply moved, declaring that the child was to him in truth a daughter (he was, I may mention, childless). He went out and brought her in to see me—a bright-eyed, delicate-looking child of about thirteen years of age appeared, whose deep filial affection for him was apparent in every gesture. When she had gone he told me he would follow the advice given by his brother and myself, and would lose no time in placing Khatiza under the latter's protection. Mahomed, who lived close by, was sent for, and in my presence accepted the trust, and in the course of a few days the girl was installed in his house, from which in the course of a few months she was well married to a

* "Reminiscences of an Indian Police Official," Chapter I.

notable in the Habsán State. In the meantime we decided that the Farreed family should offer a large reward (five hundred rupees I think was the sum) for any information that would lead to the discovery of the writers of the latest anonymous letters. The chief Magistrate's consent was obtained to my officially publishing the notification. Of course we had little hope that any reward would have results, but at any rate the notification showed that the authorities were in earnest, and that it would no longer be of any use to send anonymous letters about Abdul Farreed, while Khatiza being no longer under his roof there could be no foundation for fresh accusations. I frequently visited Abdul Farreed afterwards, and for several years afterwards, when I had left the District, we kept up a correspondence. When he was dying, some twelve years ago, he sent me a farewell message, telling me that, "thanks to me," he should die in peace. I may mention that when in great affliction about nine years ago, I received a charmingly sympathetic letter from Khatiza, who is the happy mother of a large family.

The description I have above given of the character of the Kônkanee Mussulman applies fairly well to those settled in the Deccan, but I deal with the race very fully in the two chapters that follow.

# CHAPTER XIV.

## THE DECCANEE MUSSULMAN; THE DECCAN—ACTUAL AND POSSIBLE.

### A Study in the Famine Question.—*Part I.*

I TAKE for my text the remarkable article on Cyprus by Mr. Patrick Geddes, which appears in *The Contemporary Review* for month of June last.

I wonder how many Anglo-Indian officials have taken the trouble to glance through it, much more to study and apply it to the unhappy arid zone, to the miserable population now starving in it, kept alive only by the exertion of a humane Government and the lavish generosity of the British Public.

Most Anglo-Indian students of contemporary literature, especially those who, like myself, had to do with the Famine of 1877—78 and the Locust Plague that followed—will probably have pished and pshawed testily as they came to Mr. Geddes' thoughtful paper; for they loathe—not without reason—the very name of Cyprus, associated as it is in their minds with locust driving, locust beans, carob seed, and the cultivation of mulberry trees for the revival of silk-worm breeding and silk manufacture. "Can anything good, or useful, or practical come out of Cyprus?" they say, as they skip the article. Confound historic Paphos!

"Did they (the Secretary of State for India in Council, *bien entendu*) not send us a youthful expert from the Island to teach us how to scratch up locust eggs—to circumvent the wily, agile "hoppers" before they got their wings, with trenches and sticky screens—to beat them down by myriads ere their wings had strength for flight—to

DECCANEE MUSSULMAN GENTLEMEN.

drive off the swarms of full-grown insects when they settled, on sexual pleasures intent, on the boughs of trees, with kettledrums, tom-toms, pipes, shawms, dulcimers and every kind of music? Were we not also told to take example from the Wadhárs, Mhárs and Mángs * of the Southern Maratha Country, and from the Kátkarees and forest tribes

* Low-caste tribes.

of the Kônkan who ate and fattened on locust pastry dried by the sun's powerful rays.

"Behold! it is meat for an Emperor's table," we were told—"all the same, like shrimp paste!" Did not our expert worry us with instructions innumerable? Did not a credulous Government applaud, reel off yards of Government Resolutions, dated from Bombay Castle, and revel in teaching their intellectual and more experienced equals, if not superiors, their favourite game of "How to suck eggs"? Did not the young expert settle with other official locusts at Máhábaleshwur till domestic affliction drove him to Europe, having taught us—nothing? And then a strong east wind blew all night, as in the time of Pharoah the stiff-necked, and our infernal locust pests were swept into the Indian Ocean! May the devil so fly away with their successors! and with Accountants-General and the pestilential Shylock Department, who instantly began to pester us with objections to this or that item of an expenditure which we in our hearts knew to be futile, but which His Excellency the Governor in Council hounded us on to incur! Again we say, "Confound Cyprus! we'll have no more on't."

Gently, my irate friends; "be asy"—as Pat says. Remember Kane O'Hara's appeal to the shrieking beldame!

"Pray, reader, please to moderate the rancour of your tongue.
Why flash those sparks of fury from your eyes?
Remember when the judgment's weak, the prejudice is strong!"

Behold there is not one single word about the *L. Ferox horridus* in all the Geddes article! *C'est moi qui le dit*—I've read it!

The paper you will find contains sentence after sentence strictly, marvellously applicable to the arid zone of the Deccan in which all District Officials are now, as in 1877—78, wearing out their hearts, destroying their health, shortening their lives, with no hope of receiving commendation, inspired only by duty and the dictates of humanity. In so far as their efforts may be successful, all these devoted servants of their Queen and country, all these true, best friends of the suffering peoples committed to their charge, know well that the credit will be monopolised by His Excellency the Governor, his Members in Council and any Secretariat understrappers possessed of enough impudence to push themselves forward—not one of the whole crew from H. E. downwards having had actual personal famine experience, but nevertheless guarding jealously all channels of communication with the Viceroy and the Secretary of State.

The paper also contains numerous valuable suggestions, and teems with advice, of which all in authority responsible for the management of the present calamity, responsible for the expenditure of public money and private subscriptions to the best advantage for the relief of the sufferings of to-day, for the prevention of like calamities in future, should take serious note.

By a few alterations, a few amendments, and some additions, it is easy to fit the Cypriote coat on the Deccan back; I do not doubt that the talented designer will excuse the use to which I am putting his brilliant garment. Mr. Geddes starts from Larnáke to Nicosia: let us start from Poona to Beejápoor and traverse by road and rail Máháráshtra's arid zone. *En route!*

Up from Poona, the present capital of Máháráshtra, to Beejápoor, the ancient Môgul capital, the journey most of the way is more desolate than beautiful. Yet before hurrying on, let us pause for a moment to interpret it. This desolation is the work not of nature but of man. That brazen, pitiless sky—that undulating plain o'er which ever and anon sweep fierce dust-storms in hideous mockery—that dry torrent bed—these barren hill-slopes—these skeleton hills: all go back for their explanation to the always wasteful and often wanton destruction of forest growth, which has been the crime of almost every successive race. Nowhere better can we see the lamentable way in which in these once smiling countries man has turned the forces of nature to the destruction of his home. How far the desolation and decadence so manifest in every Deccan District from the Syâdrees to the Môgulai, from Belgaum to Khándesh, is the fault of man, how far also a natural process, are questions hard to settle in exact proportion, and still likely to be long under debate; but there is no doubt of the co-operation of both destructive agencies.

Thus it is no longer a matter of speculation, but of geographical fact, that a comparison of maps and of the history of the vast area under the sway of the Âdilsháhee Dynasty a few hundred years ago, with those of to-day, shows a lamentable shrinking of tillage; vast spaces of what was then good pasture, fair arable or even rich corn land, being now represented by noxious acres of spear grass studded with exuberant clumps of poisonous cacti and stunted, profitless acacias and thorns. "How this means for the surrounding regions still hotter winds, still scantier rainfall, need hardly be explained. And though in this climatic change the ancient cycle of 'lean years and fat years' is discernible, record and observation alike show how the evil accumulates—the lean ever devouring the fat." How this continuous desiccation of the arid zone of this Presidency reacts and must continue to react on Máhá-ráshtra, alike in climate and in history, would need a volume to follow out, rather than a sentence; but broadly we may state the thesis that behind the Sirkar's (Government's) prestige, behind the anxious Empire, behind the puzzled politicians and globe-trotters of the hour, behind the dramatic detail of Famine horrors and attendant epidemics, there is going on now, as of old, the cosmic drama of geologic and climatic change. "We see how the peasant suffers from drought, but we forget that the shepherd suffers even more; we see them both driven from their ancient farms and pastures by the flaming sword of drought, the pitiless arrows of the desert sun. And as men's philosophy is the generalisation of their lives; as their religion, their theology, express its ideals, we see how there must needs have arisen in the world two main classes of religious life-theories, active and passive, as well as of life-occupations. We understand better the active Aryan, who would fain react against nature and conquer her, so that for Zoroaster

THE 'GÔLE GOOMAZ'—THE BIG DOME AT BEEJÁPOOR.
Sultan Mahmoud's Tomb.

*(See page 177.)*

he that plants a tree or digs a well fights with Ormuzd against the desert Ahriman; but we understand better also the passive submission to destiny of the Oriental religions proper, as the inevitable philosophy of the pastoral Nômad, the resignation of the peasant and the Dhangar (shepherd) overpowered by nature."

Meantime a new landscape is opening. We have crossed the hilly country, and the great Beejápoor plateau lies around us, with the dome of Sultan Mahmoud's stately tomb towering high above the landscape in solitary grandeur, just within the outer forty-mile circle of the city walls, keeping, as it were, watch and ward over the picturesque ruins of the famous City that was founded, built, flourished and destroyed within two hundred years. A date palm or two, an occasional oasis of "bâbul" (acacia) trees lighten the monotonous foreground. All around in the hazy distance crop up chains of strange little flat-topped hills, scarped away from the surrounding plateau. To the east of the squalid modern town, buried and choked in by the largest and most encroaching of the cactus tribe, rises a solitary conical hill, capped by battlements still standing in excellent preservation; at its summit a courtyard containing a handsome "peerstán" or tomb of a Mohammedan "Peer" or Saint, who first burst on an astonished world in the days of Aurungzebe, a 24 months' posthumous child (so runs the legend), full grown, bearded like a pard, clad in armour, armed to the teeth! Toiling up a long steep flight of steps cut in the solid rock, through two handsome gateways, we are received in state by the present Peer-Zádáh, or descendant of the Saint, a tall, strikingly distinguished-looking personage with the courteous high-bred mien that marks the high-born Moslem the world over. He cordially permits us to ascend to and make the circuit of the highest battlement, whence we look down on every side on as fair a view as the eye could wish to gaze upon. But 'tis a City of the Dead! Far away the circle of outer fortifications; to the West, looking towards distant Sátára, the Mahratta Gate commanded by the monster cannon "Malik-ool-Moolk" * ("The Lord of the World"), mounted on a lofty bastion, pointing toward the Mahratta foe; to the North, and stretched at our feet, the ruined walls and enclosed gardens of the old Cavalry Suburb, the favourite resort of the nobles in the good old days, studded with tombs of celebrated Commanders of the Faithful, mosques of all sizes and paved praying-places. Eighty thousand horse—history tells us—were oft-times picketed to the north, in the lines within the fortifications, and two hundred and fifty thousand people, warriors, camp-followers, grass-cutters, dancing girls, and musicians, lived a life of reckless dissipation in this suburb of Sháhpoor, now overgrown with rank vegetation—with groves of large mangoe trees, countless wild pomegranates, guavas, corrinda bushes, date palms and prickly pear. To the East the great Dome looming as if quite close at hand; to the East again, on the horizon, a long low chain of laterite hills which form the frontier of the

* See Plate, page 185.

territory of the Nizám of Hyderabad; to the south-east, far bey nd the outer walls, the fertile valley of the river Dhôn, which, tradition alleges, supplied the city of a million inhabitants with food grain in such abundance that a Mahratta ballad says, "When the Dhôn harvest is scanty, who shall eat? When the Dhôn is plenteous, who can eat

THE ÁSÁR MÁHAL.

it?" To the South, below us, the Arkilla or Inner Fortress, encircled by a broad moat—the Sât-Manzla or Seven-storied Palace towering above the battlements—the graceful, ornate "Rôza" (tomb and mosque) of Ibrahim Ádil Sháh, retired in solitary dignity, to the right, beyond it. Southward again, the outer circle of fortifications, and then the long shallow lake which in old times amply supplied the City with water under high pressure, so that a grateful fountain spouted before the Jumma Musjid, five miles distant. The glint of the sun's rays on the placid surface dazzles our vision. The broad sheet of water seems to wink in derision, as if to say, "If ye Kafirs, ye callow Civil Engineers from Cooper's Hill only knew our hidden secrets, the mysteries of our network of subterranean 'ducts, then would the dead City live again and flourish! But ye know not the things belonging to our place, and the Government of India will never give rupees enough to pay the coolies on the works, as pay them now ye must!—By the sacred hair from the Prophet's beard preserved in Ásár Máhal" (the Hall of Mirrors, or Delight) "over yonder! 'Twas little we Ádilsháhee Môguls paid for anything in our good old times! We were 'na sae blatt'—*pas si bête*, as ye say in Europe."

Biting our lips, with impatience and vexation, we turn to feast our eyes on the mid-distance with its wealth of stupendous yet graceful tombs of Kings, Mosques, Palaces, Arches, their countless domes and minarets glittering where'er we gaze. City of the Dead! we leave you with reluctance.

At my first visit to the Peer-Zádáh, I ascertained that he was in absolute penury, too proud to solicit aid, starving himself to satisfy a host of rapacious usurers, who in his father's time had gradually got hold of all the hereditary lands and allowances of the family. My informant was the hereditary Karkoon or Secretary to the "*Peerstán*", an aged Bráhmin devoted to his master, and smarting under the indignities heaped upon his honoured Chief by local Shylocks. He convinced me that with a comparatively small sum of ready money, all claims could be bought up, or compromised, and the lands being freed, the income from them would suffice in a few years, not only to pay off the loan, but to leave a sufficient income for the support of the Peer-Zádáh in dignity and comfort. Accordingly I submitted a proposal to the Government of Sir James Ferguson, who advanced the needful at small interest: the Assistant Collector was directed to superintend the management of the Estate, and to settle with all creditors; the Peer-Zádáh must long ago have been clear of debt. There are hundreds of Mahommedan gentlemen in the Deccan who could be as easily, and who ought to be, similarly succoured.

From what has preceded, the author would apostrophise the Mahommedan gentlemen of the Deccan somewhat in this fashion.

Gentlemen of the Deccan! Fanatics by religion! Fatalists by creed! Capable of truly noble and courageous deeds, yet apathetic, slothful and inert when the moment for action arises! Rouse yourselves now! *Now* is the appointed time to show yourselves superior in nobility and honour, equal in intellect and enterprise to the venomous clique who, taking advantage of your facile, listless character, are raising themselves on your degradation. They are using while they secretly abuse you.

*They* taunt *you* with lack of courage! By Allah! 'tis a shameful tale! Arise! shake off these snakes and trample them to the dust while you appeal to your true friends, the British people, who, however they may lament your faults of fanaticism and weakness, are honestly desirous of seeing you reoccupy your proper position—whose official representatives will find the means to help you if you are not too proud to state your wants. Prepare—each family—a schedule of your liabilities and your assets. Keep nothing back. Assemble at Beejápoor and memorialise the "Sirkar" to adopt for you—as it has for other communities—such measures as may be necessary for your relief from the state of impoverishment in which you have so long, so painfully existed. Then educate your youth to be useful members of society. So shall you resume your honoured place in that Deccan where you have such honourable traditions.

The Moral for the Government is obvious. A counterpoise to Bráhminical influence is needed—you have it, it is ready to your hand. Trace out the old Mahommedan families of the Deccan, and as you have restored the ancient ruined families of Guzarat, as you have helped the Peer-Zádáh of Sháhpoor, so help them, and restore an ancient aristocracy who shall in any crisis stand you in good stead, whose healthful influence shall be an antidote to Bráhminism.

# CHAPTER XV.

## THE DECCANEE MUSSULMAN *(continued)*; THE DECCAN—ACTUAL AND POSSIBLE.

### A Study in the Famine Question.—*Part 2.*

WE have left the "City of the Dead" with reluctance, as I have said above; for nowhere in all Asia better than in Beejápoor can we see the stately Môgul world with its piety and fanaticism, its culture and barbarism, its ambition and heroism; for nowhere stand nobler mosques and tombs within more skilfully designed, more gallantly defended walls. Nowhere, alas! more clear are the lapsed ideals, the corresponding material squalor of modern life, than in the hideous—where not numerous—hovels of the Deccan village, shrinking within the city walls or in the sordid lanes and shops of the modern, half Mahommedan, half Hindoo townlet spreading without, jumbled up as they are with arches that still spring light and true from noxious undergrowth and prickly pear, as from the Môgul workman's hands; and one sees with fresh clearness that architecture is not a function of paper plans, as unrolled by those clerky gentlemen we call architects in the west, for their drilled mechanics to copy, but that the masons themselves built, like bees, without architects, because they were architects, to this day the freemasons of old. There can be few more pleasing sights for any who know and care for traditional craft and individual skill. This arch-building one can see anywhere in Beejápoor. No modern British architect has possessed the genius or the audacity to emulate it.

We are gradually descending southward from the Beejápoor plateau as we traverse a desolate tract where the squalor of the villages is almost as closely associated with the prickly pear as Irish poverty with the potato. Leaving this inhospitable belt, we ride for many miles over a friable brown soil, obviously washed down from the naked hills and spurs around, of no great depth at any point, but fairly productive of the coarser food grains. The plain is dotted here and there with rich green oases of garden land, irrigated from wells and quarry holes, sunk with little labour or outlay wherever the village astrologer advised that a boring should be made. At every step we perceive what might have been, what might yet be done; and again, in the countenances and demeanour of the half-starved inhabitants we note that with the advance of disforesting and desiccation, of mutual impoverishment, comes on economic ruin.

A few miles further we encamp in a luxuriant region; fine old mango, bâbul, banyan trees rear themselves in and around fat arable fields and teeming gardens, grateful for the moisture that cools and nourishes their wide spreading roots. Such a place is Hoongoond, where we shall be

MALIK-OOL-MOOLK — THE MONARCH OF THE PLAIN.

(*See page 178.*)

taken by the impoverished descendants of a shrewd Mahommedan gentleman, to a well-shaft, driven to no great depth into solid rock till water was struck—then galleries or tunnels were driven for hundreds of yards to all points of the compass from the bottom of the shaft walls, and thus an abundant perennial supply of water was obtained. There are many such shafts and galleries in the neighbourhood, we are told, and it is plain that for many square miles there lies beneath the soil a water-bearing—one might almost term it a water-logged—rock stratum. We note the improved appearance of the villages and hamlets, the comparatively cheerful demeanour of the people, and perceive that "with water of irrigation goes ever the water of a bettered social individual life, that where there are practically no manufactures, and commerce turns on agricultural output, all reforms must come down to agriculture. So our Eastern question is ultimately an agricultural question! We see more and more clearly with Candide, '*Il faut cultiver son jardin*'." Around our gardens, too, there is ample room for the roaming flock, the half-wild shepherd. But, first of all, we must reopen ruined wells, mend broken cisterns, sink new shafts, drive new galleries into water-bearing strata, invoke the aid, profit by the advice of our Geological Department—not sneer at it and pigeon-hole its papers. "*Il faut cultiver son jardin!*"

"Thus we may read, and, if it may be, write, in silent yet living and spreading symbol, what is so hard to say in these days of futile word and unrest, that the future of the Deccan lies not in the struggle, not in the victorious or beaten isolation of its contrasted races, but in their co-operation as complementary races; not in the conflict, but in the synthesis, of its fragmentary philosophies, in such union of labour and thought as may again literally lead from the ruined well its life-giving waters, and melt also from these frozen religions their imprisoned water of life. For wherever at this moment two Easterns are quarrelling in their poverty, four or six or ten might soon be co-operating in wealth and peace. At once the actual cleansing and reopening of the ruined wells of each oasis will demonstrate this; with proportionally trifling outlay the water-supply well-nigh doubles, and with this appear new possibilities of fertility and, of course, a corresponding rise of acre-values as well," wherein a wise and liberal Sirkar (state) will benefit exceedingly, the sordid Sowkar (usurer) be discomfited, while the pestilent agitator will be deprived of his lever, the National Congress will shut up shop, the poisonous Deccan Bráhmin in his proper degraded position must feed on his own venom and sell his secret printing-press for bread. So shall peace and contentment reign throughout the land, and the prosperity of the multitude advance by leaps and bounds. So mote it be! Viceroys, Proconsuls—"prancing" or otherwise, Divisional Commissioners, hard-working Collectors and Assistant Collectors, toiling with aching hearts, choked with red tape, discouraged by apathy and pig-headedness in highest quarters: cannot this be compassed?

To you, Ministers of Indian Finance, who hold the purse-strings and guide your Shylock Department, with sardonic smiles, it may be said, Look ahead! Open your eyes bedazed with figures. Hearken to the words of the wise man and deep thinker whose paper I am so freely paraphrasing. "For the purpose of investment even, it is high time to contrast this water-mining, for which hardly any one at present cares, with the gold-mining over which all the world has run mad; time to prove, by actual results, that while the latter is on all fours with the lottery and gambling-house—in which, on the aggregate, the players and the community lose, no matter who here and there may win, and so is socially the least profitable as well as the most demoralising of all great industries,—the former is the most profitable, and that the most steadily and surely so; the most civilising and humanising also." You preen your feathers when you have floated a new loan favourably, or "converted" an old one. Strive rather to pay off old loans, by cordially encouraging schemes that palpably must lead to a "rise of acre values" and a corresponding rise in land revenue, the backbone of your finance schemes, that will prove preventives of the famines that disconcert all your well-laid plans. So will you at last produce what you have never yet attained to—a Financial Equilibrium.

To Viceroys, Governors and all Executive and Engineering Officers we will say—"Be not over ambitious; ponder on these words of experience. Help forward the incipient reaction towards a renewal of ancient, simple and economic irrigation methods, away from undue dependence on gigantic and costly engineering works. "This reaction is beginning, for instance, to be expressed by Californian or Dakotan irrigation engineers, who, after long dependence on mighty reservoirs and costly dams, on expensive artesian wells, have of late been rediscovering for themselves that 'underflow' on which most of the simple, effective and economical irrigation of antiquity and the Middle Ages was wont to depend in Cyprus and through the East."

To the present able Secretary of State for India it may be humbly suggested: Send mining geologists to note from village to village throughout the famine-stricken area, who can employ and thus teach its men to clear their own wells, to open out their springs. Send more agriculturists out, consign new seeds—(*not* through your Store Department). You little know what good has been done in this way before—"*Il faut cultiver son jardin.*'

"Ask yourself—'For social health, as for individual health, must not the essential matter be hygiene? *Il faut cultiver son jardin.* *That* is the hygiene of Peace.'

"Readers! there is no novelty in these views. Of such statements there is no lack, but one may suffice; one traditionally credited to a long and full life spent in its vortex, a life rich in observation and deep in feeling, and whose experience of action ranged from shepherd to cultivator, from victor to fugitive, from servant to king. Hear, then, the antithesis of paradise lost and paradise regained.

I.

"He turneth rivers into a wilderness and the water-springs
into dry ground,
A fruitful land into barrenness, for the wickedness of them that
dwell therein.

II.

"He turneth the wilderness into a standing water, and dry
ground into water-springs,
And there he maketh the hungry to dwell, that they may pre-
pare a city for habitation;
And sow the fields, and plant vineyards, which may yield
fruits of increase." *

* "Contemporary Review"—June 1897. Article on "Cyprus" by Mr. Patrick Geddes.

## CHAPTER XVI.

### THE TRADING CLASSES—THE AGRICULTURAL AND RURAL, THE ARTIZAN CASTES.

THE trading classes naturally include Hindoos from all parts of Hindostan: bankers and money-lenders, all known as Sowkars, who may be Bráhmins of any sect; or Goozurs and Wánees from Guzarat; or Bháttias from Kutch; or Márwárrees from Káthiawar and Râjpootána. All these undertake ordinary banking business; all deal in agricultural produce; all lend money on usury; of all, worse even than the Márwárree, the Bráhmin is the closest-fisted, the greatest skinflint, while he is the most timid of traders.

The Bráhmin Sowkar finds time to engage in a hundred intrigues, domestic, legal, social and political, while he retains a merciless grip on the luckless peasantry.

The *Goozar* or *Wánee* is absorbed in money-getting—he cares naught for politics—he goes to law to recover money or money's worth—he intrigues to make money and for nothing else—he has some bowels of compassion for his creditor, and is proverbially charitable.

The Bháttia is usually the representative or agent of some large wholesale firm in Bombay, and has again his petty agents, brokers and "dulals" buying up produce or "placing" bales of piece-goods with retail dealers in every town and hamlet. He is absolutely, blissfully ignorant of politics—his eye is fixed on the markets; he rarely troubles the Civil Courts, seeing no wisdom in throwing good money

THE WÁNEE OR GOOZUR.

after bad. He too is very charitable, usually kind, often indeed generous, to his employés.

The Márwárree is a curious combination of Shylock and Harpagon. All is fish that comes to his net – he is a bold speculator and will venture his money to people of all races and castes, long after other Sowkars have refused credit; he exacts his pound of flesh to the last shred and is therefore a great patron of the law Courts; he takes care to be well informed of the trend of public feeling,

THE MÁRWÁRREE.

not that he cares a jot for politics, but because well he knows that should disturbances arise, he will probably be the first to suffer in person as well as property. Márwárrees are really aliens of Poona and Máháráshtra because they have their homes in Márwár Rajpootana and Central India, and take or remit their savings to those homes. They are traders, some of them on a large scale, in cloth and grain, in gold and silver, but the majority of them are usurers pure and simple.

THE KHOJAH.

Taken as usurers they are not bad fellows—at least they compare favourably with your English Kirkwoods *et hoc genus:* they usually syndicate their loans, especially when their client is a European: they never charge less than 24 per cent, often 60 per cent, and they usually get paid. They do pawnbroking on a small scale, and will speculate in anything that promises a quick return. They are not charitable, though they have been known to be guilty (from their point of view) of very generous dealings, especially towards Englishmen.

In common with all traders they rub their noses, remembering how in the good old days Raghojee Bhángria and

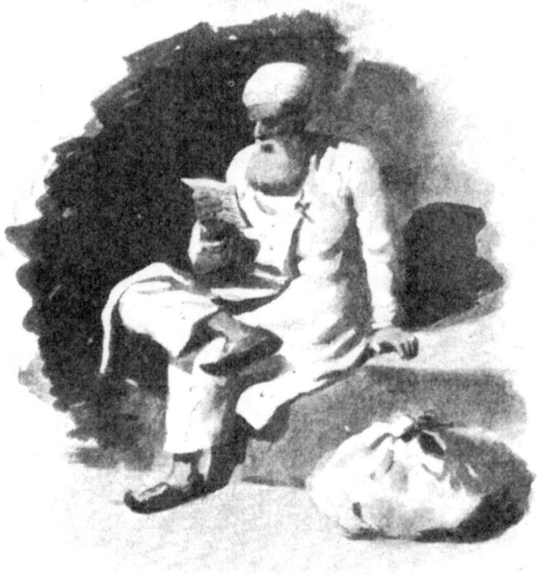

THE BORAH.

Bhágojee Naique used to send them by scores to the hospital with no nasal organs worth mentioning.

### THE SHOPKEEPING CLASSES.

Shopkeepers are shopkeepers all the world over, but in the City of Poona it is remarkable how Mahommedans, and Hindoos, Khôjahs and Borahs, "Moochees" (Shoemakers), Chámbars or Curriers, Kátiks or Mahratta Butchers, Sweetmeat sellers and petty grocers, work amicably together. Above all, the hardware dealers have flourished exceedingly during the past 40 years. The writer remembers the time that the only hardware retail shop in the Western Presidency was that of Mr. Walker, the well-known "Tom Cringle" of Bombay journalism. *Now* there must be at least fifty Khôjah and Borah firms with their own travellers on the continent, so articles "made in Germany" are very numerous, cheap—and flimsy. These followers of the Prophet are very charitable to their own people—but the charity of the Wánee, Bháttia and Goozar shopkeeper is extended to all classes.

## THE AGRICULTURAL AND LABOURING AND RURAL CASTES.

### THE 'KOONBEES', 'RYOTS', OR CULTIVATORS.

Megasthenes, a writer quoted by Strabo and Arrian, who was an *attaché* of Syburtius, Governor of the Arachosii on the Sáraswatee more than three thousand years ago, described the husbandman or Koonbee "as amongst the most numerous and mildest of all classes, who do not resort to cities, or take part in public tumults. It therefore frequently happens that at the same time and in the same part of the country, one body of men are in battle array, while others are ploughing and digging in security, leaving the soldiers to protect them. The whole of the territory belongs to the King (or ruler); the husbandmen cultivate it, on paying three-fourths of the produce." * This description holds good now, except that the Koonbee only pays one-sixth of the produce (or its value) to the State, and that he does now sometimes enlist in the army and engage as labourer in mills and other industries.

Koonbees usually do not marry till some time after puberty: their attachment to their homes, to their own particular fields is proverbial: whatever a Koonbee away from home can manage to scrape together he brings or sends to his family in his native village. Frugal, industrious, patient and long-suffering, he toils from dawn to sundown in all weathers, while his women-folk grind the poorest grains, bake the coarse cakes, collect sticks, manufacture cow-dung cakes for fuel, and fetch water all the day long from year's end to year's end, only visiting the towns or cities on market days to dispose of their surplus produce, to buy or sell a bullock, to pay the Sowkar (or money-lender) or to pass another bond. Then the wife buys perhaps a cheap "sarree" or petticoat, perhaps a few glass bangles or brass ornaments, may be a scarlet jacket for little Bappoo making dirt pies at home. There is mirth and contentment that night in the dearly loved mud hut, unless indeed—as now too often happens—the husband has taken a little too much "phènee" (native liquor), when the Bye's (wife's) shrill voice will be heard in objurgation till the neighbours make peace between the hapless pair.

* Wilson's *Indian Caste*. Vol. I, p. 344.

On the whole the Koonbees, if they do not live a very eventful life, if their household property consists only of a few brass pots and pans, their furniture one "charpoy" or four-footed cot, a couple of low stools and perhaps a swing in the verandah, pass fairly happy—certainly con-

THE KOONBEE OR RYOT, IN THE RAINS.

tented—lives. Their wants are very small in food or raiment, their shelter is their own; they have not the constant dread —as their forefathers had—of being looted by this or that official, by the ruffians fighting for neighbouring chieflets, or by other bands of robbers; they live in peace, their chief anxiety being how to stave off the rapacious

Sowkar, how to find cash to pay the Sirkar's next revenue instalment. Though they no longer bury their surplus grain in pits because they cannot sell it—for they now have easily accessible markets by good roads—they have wonderful staying power in bad seasons, and if the worst comes to

COOLY, BIGARREE, OR PORTER.

the worst and famine threatens, they now know by experience that the Sirkar (Government) will do its level best to mitigate their sufferings. Let no one in England believe that this class, "the most numerous and the mildest" in Máháráshtra, are discontented or ripe for rebellion.

### THE COOLIES, BIGÁRREES, PORTERS AND DAY-LABOURERS.

This useful class are usually Koonbees, but those employed about the market are mostly Mhárs.

The capacious baskets which they carry on their heads will hold anything, from a live sheep to a dozen tins of groceries and a pile of fruit and vegetables—when the load is larger, as a portmanteau or box, the basket is clapped on the top. They will work about your garden or in your house by day or hour, are often very handy, like the "odd men" of England, but much more willing, honest, and hard-working.

### THE GOWLEES OR MILKMEN.

The Gowlee or Milkman because of his association with the sacred animal, naturally occupies a high position among the Shudras, taking rank immediately below the Koonbee in the orthodox scheme of castes. The consumption of milk in all its forms in and around the City of Poona must be enormous, seeing that at least half the population consume it largely as milk, in curds or buttermilk, as ghee or clarified butter. It is drawn principally from buffaloes, large herds of which are tended in the environs of the City. The fluid is brought in morning and afternoon from the grazing grounds, in large brass "lotahs" (crocks), placed one atop of another and then attached to each end of a stout pole, which the Gowlee, balancing on his shoulder, trots off with to the City,—frothing or spilling being prevented by a wisp of straw, grass or herbs stuck in the pot. The milk is sold off at once, and boiled by the purchaser.

They are many thousands of milch buffaloes round Poona, and half as many men and women are engaged in the trade. The Gowlee has not the best of reputations for honesty, and is believed, not without reason, to be in the

GOWLEES OR MILKMEN.

habit of poisoning the cattle of rival dealers or of private individuals, especially Europeans, Parsees and Mahommedans, who keep their own cattle so as to be sure of sweet new milk. The writer has never heard that the Gowlees have been concerned in anything more heinous, or that they are discontented. They certainly have no cause to be so.

### THE MALEES OR GARDENERS.

With a population like that in Poona, needing fruit and flowers in every domestic ceremony, for offerings to the gods, for garlands and nosegays for every guest, for presents to superiors: with a strong local and commercial demand for sugar, and an insatiable market for fruit and vegetables in the great city of Bombay, it follows that the Malees are well-to-do. Most of them are Mahrattas of the upper classes—many of them are connected with the best Mahratta families—not a few of them are wealthy to a moderate extent—all are contented, and are incapable of harbouring seditious thoughts.

### THE DHUNGARS OR SHEPHERDS AND HERDSMEN.

The Shepherd begins his season after the rains, about the Dussera, when he betakes himself far away into the Mogulai or Nizám's country where he begins to form the nucleus of a flock of sheep and goats, or to buy to replenish that he has been grazing on waste lands or as best he could near home during the hot weather. Gradually increasing his stock, he drives slowly down to Poona, or by Nassick to Bombay, grazing the flocks as they go and being paid in grain—a seer or two per score or hundred—till he reaches rice stubble-lands, where he not only feeds but pens on selected seed plots, for which he is paid right well. He buys a pony here and a bullock there, till he reaches a good grain market, with quite a little train of pack animals heavily laden with grain of all sorts; then he sells the lot, grain and beasts, and hies him to Bandora slaughter-houses with his bleating flock. He is probably under contract with commissariat agents at Poona or Egutpoora, and drops them the fattest animals as he passes. He is also probably under advances from Bombay butchers. The writer has often met

THE DHUNGAR OR SHEPHERD.

him in the Kônkan, with two or three thousand rupees in currency notes. Heaven knows what he does with his money, for he is always as Mr. van Ruith here depicts him, seemingly as poor as Job! He encamps on the outskirts of Poona City and never enters it but to sell his grain and to buy some condiments or strong drinks. He is quite harmless—rather a misanthrope withal, and certainly the very last man to mix himself up with politics, or Deccan Sabha movements.

There are besides, the Dhungar herdsmen who graze herds of horned cattle on the mountains and forests, but these never come to Poona at all. Reducing the milk to "ghee" or clarified butter, and storing it in leathern "dubbas" or jars, they sell it to dealers with whom they are usually under contract.

THE NHÁWEE—HAJAM—OR BARBER.

The Nháwees of the city and the Hajáms of the civil and military station are of the same caste, but the latter from their association with Europeans are the better men. They have latterly been carrying on a kind of revolt against the Bráhmins, the precise nature of which I have forgotten, but it has something to do with their caste ceremonies and Bráhmin fees, and it is, or was, headed by a very independent Nháwee family in Joonere, near Poona. They are intelligent, and, like Figaros all the world over, garrulous, the purveyors of all the gossip of the countryside. The Nháwees are much belied if they do not, like the barber of Seville, act as go-betweens in many a love intrigue. The Hajáms, on the other hand, are extremely proper and often amusing. When one does not expressly stipulate that one's hair is to be cut in solemn silence, one will be regaled with something like the following:—"Smith Sahèb's Mem's Ayah run away last night, with Bootler (butler)—take all mem Sahèb's jewels and Sahèb's guns. Poona Pōlis never catch, they all pájee fellows (rogues themselves);" or, "General Sahèb very 'ghoossa' (angry) on parade this morning. Sepoy Phulthans (Regiments) not 'chul' (march) quick! Colonel Sahèb's much wigging get. Sepoy leave stop – this bazaar 'gup' (rumour)," and so on as long as the patient chooses. But who does not know good Old Tom the Barber! Tom, by the way, is the very last person to communicate anything but stale news of the City, for the best of reasons—he never hears any till 'tis stale!

### THE GÂBEETS—FISHERMEN—BOODEE-MARS OR DIVERS.

These are very numerous in and around Poona by reason of the two rivers Moota and Moolla, in which there are deep "dows" or reaches teeming with fish, large and small. Some of them, mostly the old men and boys, content themselves with casting, purse, and spoon nets, in which they catch the smaller fry at the mouths of brooks, or at any point where the stream narrows or can be contracted into a rapid. The able-bodied, fine, well-grown jovial fellows work in large gangs with long deep nets.

Their mode of proceeding is as follows:—Selecting a suitable point in a "dow", they net it across from bank to bank, and then forming in line at the head of a pool,

each man with a long pole, and with inflated skins under his arms, they advance shoulder to shoulder towards the net, treading water and striking their poles down vertically on the bed of the river. Thus they disturb the large fish at the bottom and drive them forward to the net, which has one or more long purses. When close to the net, discarding their floats and poles, they dive and kill the fish entangled in the meshes: finally, the whole length of the net, which is a cross between the drag net and flue used in England, is hauled up on one bank, and the purse emptied of its finny contents. The fish, most of them of the carp and barbel species, run to an enormous size and realise good prices in the City.

In much the same way they are employed by the authorities to recover the bodies of persons drowned—they never fail to find where the drags have been unsuccessful.

The Mucheemárs are good fellows, good-tempered and law-abiding, quarrelsome only in their cups, and then only among themselves.

### THE BHUNDÁREES OR TODDY DRAWERS.

These come from the Kônkan, where they tend the cocoanut and betel (sooparee) palms, but numbers of them have spread into the Deccan. They are employed on the railways as porters and gatekeepers, and in the police, but they rarely enlist in the regular army, possibly because most of them, though broad in the chest and with immense muscular development of the legs and arms, are below the military standard in height. They are a somewhat stolid, but good-natured race, very active and industrious, fairly intelligent and notoriously trustworthy and honest.

If they do not wear much clothing when climbing up and down their trees, it is because clothes would be in the way. Off duty they are particularly fond of bright colours and finery. A Bhundáree decked out in his gala dress, with a turban as broad as a cartwheel set jauntily on one side of his head, heavy ear-rings, broad silver "kirgootee" or waist-belt, and a showy shawl, is a goodly sight;

BHUNDÁREES.

Their women are quite as addicted to gaudy decoration, and are said to be particularly virtuous.

Bhundárees, however, are decidedly but harmlessly bumptious and conceited: so there is a Mahratta saying, "Bhundáree záteet akud phar!" which means "There is much coxcombry in the Bhundáree caste"; or, "Bhundárees are very cocky."

A Bhundáree once your friend is always your friend, once put in a position of trust he never betrays it, and he is truthful as Hindoos go.

### THE ARTISAN CLASSES.

"Sônars" or goldsmiths head the artisan classes. From a Bráhmin by a "Shudra" wife was born a "Nisháda" or goldsmith, so says the Reverend Dr. Wilson; but he adds in a note (vol. 1, page 56): "The Bombay goldsmiths, however, do not like to be associated with the Nishádas, and plead for being considered a sort of sub-Bráhmin. The 'Syadree Khanda' gives to the Sônar more than the religious status of a Shudra. It denominates him as a 'Máháshudra' or great Shudra." Sônars are far and away the best of the Shudras: from time immemorial they have been renowned for their shrewdness and integrity, for the beauty and vivacious intelligence of their women, whom they have always educated and treated as equals. Some of the caste have risen, are still rising, and will continue to rise in the social scale. Jugonath Sunkersett of Bombay, the great philanthropist, was a Sônar, who earnestly hoped that he would be admitted to the Bráhminical caste. Many of them are in the Government service, and the State never had a more able financier and accountant than Nágoba Sónaba, whom the writer first knew as head accountant at

Satára, 40 years ago. The working goldsmith whom my friend Van Ruith depicts, is of a humbler class. He is to be trusted with untold wealth, and with the simple implements around him it is simply marvellous what exquisite and artistic work he will produce. There are those among

'ORKING SÔNAR OR GOLDSMITH

them who have been led away to copy European designs which are, no doubt, faithful copies, but they are not art.

| | | |
|---|---|---|
| "Tambhars" | = | Coppersmiths, |
| "Kánsars" | = | Braziers, |
| "Lôhars" | = | Blacksmiths, |
| "Sootars" | = | Carpenters |

may all be classed together—with the note that "Lôhars"

and "Sootars" intermarry; in fact it is not uncommon to find both carpenters and blacksmiths in the same family.

The metal work now executed in Poona cannot be excelled even in Benáres—but the fear is that, like Benáres, Poona may adopt the emasculated models supplied by

THE SHIMPEE OR TAILOR.

Birmingham. Many of these castes are becoming good mechanics and engineers in the railway and mill workshops.

## SHIMPEES OR TAILORS.

Time was—not so many years ago—when the Shimpee was an honoured and influential personage in the City; there are still many of tho old school as depicted above, who work themselves, with only male assistants, and fashion the quaint garments that still adorn old-fashioned people, but they are being superseded by operators on "Singers" and other sewing-machines, which will be heard at work in every street. It is in India, however, as it is in England: ask any native which he prefers, which is more

MÓOCHEE OR SHOEMAKER.

durable, the machine-made garment or the hand-stitched? The answer will be the same. There are many Shimpees in Poona who have amassed wealth and are held in high consideration.

## MOOCHEE OR SHOEMAKER.

These are low castes, of course, from the nature of their occupation necessitating the handling of dressed skins. They earn good wage and would be well off but that they drink heavily and can never be depended on to finish a job. Madrassees and Chinamen now compete keenly with them in all large towns.

# CHAPTER XVII.

## THE OUT CASTES.—THE HILL OR WILD TRIBES. THE MIGRATORY OR PREDATORY TRIBES.

### OUT CASTES.—THE MHÁRS.

WITHOUT doubt the Mhárs are, as they claim to be, the aboriginal inhabitants of Máháráshtra, though Bráhmins assert otherwise. It would be difficult even now for the country to get on without them. The Mhár—sometimes called the Dhèr, "Bhoomia" or guide, Yèshkur or watchman, "Tural" or gatekeeper—is the very first man appealed to, whether it be about a murder or robbery, a burglary, or a boundary dispute. He is the incarnation of the traditions and history of his village, and though he is despised, condemned to live outside the village, and fearful of letting his defiling shadow fall on the Bráhmin, the latter well knows he can do nothing without him. He holds lands—the worst in the village—on hereditary tenure: he is entitled by prescription (which has often been affirmed in the Law Courts) to certain grain allowances, of which he is as often as not deprived. A stranger or a traveller comes—"Mhárálá Boláwá" (call the Mhár). A robbery occurs—"Mhárás wichyárá" (ask the Mhár). Who owns this field? What are the boundaries? "Mhárás máhit ahè" (the Mhár knows)—and so on.

In all Máháráshtra there is no class on the whole so reliable, so trusty, so honest, so hardworking as the despised Mhár. Look at the records of old Infantry Regiments—look at some of the muster rolls now—look at the pension

MHÁRS.

rolls, and you will find the names of Soobedúr Majors, Sirdar Bahadoors—Rámnaks—Yèsnaks—Bhágnaks and all the "Náks." Ask in the Kônkan, "By whom was this road made? by whom this bridge, this school, or rest-house, or Sahèb's bungalow built?" The answer will be—"By Mhárs." Ask any British officer of any service, who makes the best "ghorawalla" or horsekeeper? who was his most reliable servant in any arduous expedition? The answer will be "Báloo Mhár."

In large cities they are the scavengers—are shamefully neglected and left to rot and die, as in the city of Poona at the present moment.

## THE MHÁNGS.

The Mháng is the lowest of the low, and is—or was—often driven to dacoity by starvation. He gets the hides of dead animals, (he eats the carcases,) and makes raw-hide ropes and reins, and thongs of whips for cartmen. It was his duty in old days to carry out executions, and if no one else were available (a Chinaman, to-wit) in a gaol, he would be the hangman now. He will disappear as the world grows older.

## THE HILL OR WILD TRIBES.—THE RÁMOOSHEES OF THE GHAUTS AND OF THE EUROPEAN STATION.

The Rámooshees of the Ghauts are a hill-tribe, inhabiting the sterile spurs and valleys on the western face of the Syadrees, near Poona. They are not now naturally badly disposed, and they are as easily influenced for good as for evil, but they are bitterly poor,—bad cultivators, the land they cultivate is heart-breakingly unproductive. Their traditions are of robbery and rapine, committed often to get the means to live; as often as not they are the tools of dishonest or vindictive Bráhmins and receivers, who select their victims for them, receive their booty, cheat them in paying for it, and when a crisis comes, betray them to the police. They do not ordinarily visit the City of Poona, nor are many of them resident on its outskirts, but when any considerable number are observed in Poona, the authorities ought to be very sure that some desperate enterprise is afoot. There have been useful Rámooshee semi-police corps, and

RÁMOOSHEE OF THE STATION.

one might be raised again and employed at a distance from their homes, where they must always be at starvation point for three or four months preceding the first harvest of their poor hill crops. The Rámooshees of the civil station and cantonment are another sort of watchmen. Certain it is that if you do not keep a Rámooshee for night guard round your house, you run a great risk of being robbed. He may be a Purdàsee, a Mhàr, a low-class

Mussulman, or even a Mhàng, but have one you must. Enveloped in a thick "kumblee" or coarse blanket, with the dirtiest wisp of cloth wound round his head, some Sahèb's old waistcoat or jacket on his body, a "langoti" or loin cloth, perhaps a pair of Sahèb's breeches—perhaps not—and a pair of sandals, he perambulates your garden with a long staff in hand, striking it anon on the ground, and giving vent at intervals to a sepulchral cough. Dogs do not bark at him, cats flee from him, owls and bats wheel familiarly round his head; your "nôkar lôg" (servants) to a man and woman—keep on the best of terms with him by reason of his knowing of all their little nocturnal games and peccadilloes.

He learns and knows many secrets, does the Rámooshee, and, like Mr. Tulkinghorn, he dislikes to share them with anybody.

So soon as it is daylight he rolls himself up in some shed or outhouse for two or three hours of solid sleep, after which he may be seen—and heard – gurgling and clearing his throat cheerfully in the shadow of his lair. He is as honest as may be, at any rate he prevents any outsider from robbing you.

I purposely refrain from describing the Bheels, Kôlees, and Kátódees of the Ghauts, because the two first tribes inhabit the Syadrees to the North of the Rámooshees' hills; and the last the Western or Kônkan side of the great range of mountains—none of them frequent the city of Poona.

THE PHÁNSI PÁRDEES OR GAME SNARERS.

### THE MIGRATORY AND PREDATORY TRIBES.

Their number is legion.

"*Oochlias*" * and "*Bamptias*".—Thieves and pickpockets, who do nothing but steal, and never will do anything else.

"*Kaikáris*" and "*Booroods*".—Basket-makers and mat-weavers, who do some work, and the latter are fairly honest.

"*Bèldars*" and "*Pâtroots*".—Quarrymen and stone-dressers, who are expert burglars, but very hardworking.

"*Phánsi Párdees*" or game snarers, who snare game; they may be met with poles on which are perched rows of live pea-fowl with their eyes sewn up, and baskets of live quail and partridges. They are the abomination of the sportsman, and know no seasons.

"*Waddárs*" or earth workers—the navvies of Western and Southern India, who have made most of the earth embankments of all the railways. These have been reclaimed from evil courses by honest and highly remunerative industry; they take petty contracts by the thousand "bras" or 100 cubic feet. They have an honourable future, and are on the whole good fellows.

There are a host of others—some workers—some altogether thieves—all horribly filthy in their habits, in their persons and in their food. All their women are prostitutes of the very lowest type, and loathsome diseases decimate them, for they all drink. They are not permitted to enter any town or village, so camp outside, and let loose their donkeys

* From "Oochalne"—"to pick up."

and buffaloes at night to graze at their sweet will on the people's crops. Catch them who can! the beasts are as knowing as their owners, and village pounds will not hold them. These various races, who do not intermarry, are dying out—may we say "a good riddance of bad rubbish"?

## TÁMÁSHA WALLAS OR SHOWMEN.

Jugglers, Acrobats, Conjurers, Dancers and Musicians are of course very numerous around (for they rarely camp in) the City of Poona. Mr. Van Ruith has given a charming picture of a gang about to begin business in a suburb. There are of course musicians and dancers of a much higher class who are regularly employed in the City for "nautches" and other high-class entertainments; of their morals the less said the better. Not much more can be said of the women-kind of the lower classes who purvey for public amusement. The honesty of all is decidedly questionable; they are educated enough to make a good deal of money occasionally by blackmailing respectable or ostensibly respectable citizens.

In olden days these people used to follow in the rear of Môgul armies and have what "'Arry" calls "a 'igh old time"! In a defeat they changed sides easily and marched with the victors. In the present day, should these festive gangs somewhat suddenly leave the City, let the Police be on the *qui vive*, for most certainly there is going to be a riot or a row of some kind.

TÁMÁSHA WALLAS—MUMMERS—SHOWMEN AND JUGGLERS.

THE GÔSÁEES OR RELIGIOUS DEVOTEES.

I purposely include these among the Predatories because they mostly prey on other people for their subsistence. Otherwise they are very holy men, and are regarded with great veneration, or rather with superstitious dread, by all classes.

A GÔSÁEE.

They are followers of "Mhádeo". The majority of them are by no means ascetics; on the contrary, some are very wealthy traders and bankers. They have played an important part in Mahratta history, and have fought like tigers on many occasions, notably in Sindia's armies.

15

They were also invaluable as spies and informers in days gone by. An interesting history of a Gôsáee is to be found in Sir Bartle Frere's "Pandoorang Hurree", and Meadows Taylor often mentions them also. The individuals who distort and contort their limbs and voluntarily undergo incredible torture are probably half-witted fanatics. An efficient detective police force ought to have several Gôsáees in its ranks and in its pay. The indecent and very mal-odorous gentleman depicted on the preceding page will be recognised by many Anglo-Indians.

# CHAPTER XVIII.

## THE ALIEN INHABITANTS OF POONA.—THE PARSEES.

THE history of this enterprising race is well worthy of study. In this notice, however, I must necessarily confine myself to their connection with Poona and the Deccan where they have settled and are prospering in considerable numbers. Their "prosperity may be said to date from their first connection with the English, and still more precisely from the time of their settlement in Bombay", in 1668. There were energetic Parsees, however, in Bombay before the island was given by the King of Portugal to England as the dowry of Catherine of Braganza, on her marriage with Charles II.; for one Kharshedji Panday contracted with the Portuguese Government for men and materials for the Bombay fortification.

The first Parsee who appears in the history of the Deccan was Kharshedji Jamshedji Modi *—he originally came from Cambay, and as a young man was taken into his office by Colonel Close, the Resident at Poona; exceptionally intelligent and energetic, and possessed in an eminent degree of that tact which enables Parsees under any circum-

* Otherwise called Khoosroojee Mody.

stances "to live on good terms with other races with whom they happen to be brought in contact, no matter how different their creeds and customs," Karshedji Modi was promoted in 1809 to the post of native agent. In this capacity he necessarily had much intercourse with Bájee Rao, the last of the Peishwas; and Bájee Rao, not only consulted him on

PARSEES—LADY AND GENTLEMAN.

all important questions, but also appointed him, with a large salary, to the post of Sur-Soobha or Governor of the Carnatic, a post which he held at the same time as he filled that of native agent under the English Resident.

Modi in this extraordinary dual position of trust, was thoroughly faithful to both the British and to the Mahratta

Court. He built himself a house on the edge of a watercourse, half-way between the "Sungum" (British Residency) and the walls of Poona city. It was at this very nullah or watercourse, and all around the Modi's bungalow, that Bájee Rao's cavalry under Phadkay, were checked in their charge on the little British Force assembled on the battlefield of Kirkee, behind it. It was within a few yards of this bungalow that poor Mr. Rand and Lieutenant Ayerst were treacherously done to death on the Diamond Jubilee night. (*Vide* Illustration, page 9—Modi's house is visible to the right.)

"It was of course impossible in any native Government for an alien to hold high office without exciting the envy of the officers of the State, and one of the Peishwa's Sardars, Seodáseo Bhow Mánkèshwur, preferred charges against Kharshedji Modi, of corrupt practices in the affairs of his Government, but the Peishwa took no steps to investigate them. Another of Bájee Rao's Sardars, the infamous Trimbuckjee Danglià, informed Mr. Mountstuart Elphinstone, who was then Resident at Poona, that Kharshedji was conspiring with Bájee Rao against the English." Mr. Elphinstone justly considered that Kharshedji's position at the Residency was incompatible with his appointment as Governor of a Mahratta province, and he was called upon to resign the one or the other. Kharshedji knew what was good for an honest man, and he stuck to his less lucrative post in the English service, and resigned the higher office under the Peishwa." The intrigues against him were renewed in different forms, and he was at length removed from the Residency, but with a handsome provision for him in his native country. Before he could leave Poona, however, he died (1815) of poison, but whether administered by others or taken by himself, was never ascertained.

After the battle of Kirkee (1818) Parsee traders of all kinds came up to the Deccan from Bombay and Guzerat. One family, the Cursetjis, had already accompanied (1803) Sir Arthur Wellesley to, and settled at, Ahmednuggur as merchants and shopkeepers. They have now branch establishments at Kirkee and all the principal towns. The best Police Inspector in the Deccan was Khán Bahadoor Framji Cursetji of Ahmednuggur City. Cursetji and Sons for nearly a century past have been the best friends of poor English officers, their wives and families, in the hour of need or sickness. God reward them!

The Viccaji family, hailing from Tárápur in the Thanah District, after farming the land and sea customs in the Kônkans (1836) took up similar farms in Poona, Sholapar, Ahmednuggur and Khandeish. Members of the family had already found their way into the Nizám's dominions. They were the first (1825—26) to export cotton from the Berárs. They erected the first cotton screws and presses at Khângaum and in the neighbouring cotton districts. They made cart roads over the Ghauts, and built bridges on the route from the Deccan to the coast. Finally, under the Nizám's Prime Minister, Rájá Chandoo Làl, they established their banking firm of "Pestomji Viccaji" at Hyderadad, and financed the Nizám's Government for many years; the State

LADY JAMSETJI'S DAM AT POONA.

(*See page 233.*)

Mint at Aûrungabàd was under their charge. Within one decade (1835 to 1845) they advanced more than a million sterling to the Nizám. Chandoo Làl retired from office in 1845, and his successor, Rájá Ràmbax, refusing to settle with the Viccaji Firm for the modest sum of three hundred and seventy-five thousand pounds, proceeded in true Mogulai fashion to sequestrate the Provinces that had been mortgaged to them. The Firm of course appealed, first to the Government of India, then to the Court of Directors, lastly to the House of Commons, and were as a matter of course refused redress, on the sound principle, applied to the case of the Palmers (also large creditors of the Nizám), that British subjects advanced moneys to Native States at their own risk, and must not expect the British Government to aid them in recovering their debts. The family were practically ruined from that time, but Sir Sálar Young, with characteristic nobility, took several of its members into the Nizám's employ, and made a sufficient provision for the family from the State Exchequer.

The Jamsetji Jeejeebhoy family, the acknowledged heads of the Parsee race, of course soon made their mark in Poona. It was in 1841—42 that Lady Jamsetji expended some £16,000 on the Bund or Dam over the river Moolla, which has saved so many lives and contributed in no small degree to the health of the City of the Peishwas. (*Vide* Illustration, p. 231.)

The Padamji family rose later to eminence. The founder, Khán Báhádur Padamji Pstomji, is the actual head of the

Parsee Community in Poona. His great services as Mail Contractor during the Mutinies were appropriately rewarded by the Viceroy by a gold medal and the title of Khán Báhádur, and in latter years by the enrolment of his name among the first-class Sardars of the Deccan. His sons have trodden successfully and honourably in their father's footsteps, have been distinguished in science and photography, have founded and managed the Poona Paper Mills, and Mr. Dorabji Padamji for many years held his own as one of the best rifle shots in India.

Parsee ladies, wherever they are to be found in the Deccan, as in Bombay, are distinguished for their refinement and culture, for their virtue and domesticity, as for their beauty. It is believed that they deeply deplore the gulf that has been opened between their people and their best and oldest friends, the English, by reason of the folly of a few of their younger male relatives who have been led away to join the National Congress. The writer knows that Parsee ladies have striven to restrain and to reclaim the headstrong youths, and that it is their influence that prevents the spread of Bráhmin poison among their race.

Needless to say that no Parsee name is to be found at the foot of the seditious so-called petitions and memorials which preceded the Jubilee murders; the Poona and Deccan Anglo-Parsee Press has always been admirable in its tone, if somewhat weak in its language. It is capable in able Parsee hands, of exercising a very powerful influence for good in the Deccan, as it already does in Bombay and Gujerat.

The author would earnestly exhort the Parsee race somewhat in the following terms:—

"Citizens of the world! Pioneers in distant lands, in commerce, in manufacture; far-seeing, enterprising; liberal and generous in promoting every scheme that holds out fair promise of developing the resources of the countries you explore, of benefiting the human race—and filling your own pockets *bien entendu!* * Your race can still play a much nobler part in cosmic history. Train your young men to agriculture, to geology, to water-mining, as you already train them to trade, to mechanics, to engineering. Leave law, license of speech, evil speaking (and writing), lying and slandering to that knot of wily Bráhmins licensed to these pursuits by Secretaries of State, Viceroys and Governors! Let these dogs of the Deccan delight to bark and bite, but do not bay with them; rather aid the Sirkar to hunt them down in their lairs! Eschew Politics! Think of your history, past and present! What possible concern have Parsees with Politics? What business have they to join National Congresses? Withdraw your few names from this roll of rascals ere it be too late and your vast majority of loyal British subjects become befouled by Bráhminical influences! Misguided few! attracted by a treacherous will-o'-the-wisp exhaling from the foetid swamp of 'twice-born' discontent. Can you not see, triple asses

* Why not?

that you are! that you are being made cat's-paws of by these green-eyed monsters, who bite the hand that educated, fed and fondled them, who systematically repay benefits by treachery, rear their heads defiantly when they dare, fawn, flatter and intrigue when they dare not. *Leave them to God: He* will, *He* is punishing that venomous clique. It is doomed to decay, disgrace, destruction, like Sodom and Gomorrah of old!"

A few words of humble counsel of the Powers that be as to their treatment of Parsees of the present generation.

If you have on the roll of your officials young Parsees who have displayed National Congress proclivities, give them their *congé*. They cannot be trusty servants of the State.

On the other hand, relax your rigid rules for admission into the Revenue and Magisterial service. The Government never had a better Revenue officer than the late Pestomji Jehanghir, not to mention many other Parsee gentlemen, some few of whom are still languishing in subordinate Revenue posts.

Recruit your higher Police grades from Parsees—especially your Detective department *when you have one* *. Khán Báhádur Framji Nusserwanji Cursetji of Admednuggur: Khán Sahèb Framji Narimon of Kolába, Habsân, and Belgaum—the Inspector Bucket of the author's time—would long ago have run in the Jubilee murderers and their instigators. Parsees possess the requisite qualifications of detectives in an eminent degree, by reason of their tact and energy,

* When will that be? See Chapter XX.

because (as their historian aptly puts it) "they invariably live on good terms with other races, no matter how different their creeds and castes," because they "always adapt themselves to circumstances," because they "possess the happy knack of getting on well with everybody." (*Vide* Introduction of the admirable *History of the Parsees*, by Dossabhai Framji Káráka, p. xvii.)

### THE MOODLIAR (MADRASSEE.)

There are but few families of these Madrassee gentlemen resident in Poona, as bankers or merchants: they would not be noticed but for the fact that an amiable and respectable, but not too intelligent member of the little community signed that notable memorial previous to the Jubilee murders, which certain members of Parliament cited as proving that the people of Poona had been driven to desperation by the plague operations. The signatory was afterwards stated by the eccentric member for Banffshire to belong to one of the richest mercantile firms in the City (which was inaccurate) and to possess great influence (which he does not). The "Pooh-pooh Swamys" have no influence and represent nobody. The Moodliars settled in Poona as Commissariat and Military Transport Contractors, in which capacities they did excellent service, and amassed moderate fortunes. They are kindly, charitable, easy-going, anxious to show public spirit, but, lacking backbone, they are certain to be fooled by local agitators, like others who cannot, like them, plead ignorance. It was crafty, Bráhmin-like of the Poona Sabha to get this signature as one of the five members of the Memorial Committee; but the falsity of this document

THE MOODLIAR.

has been so thoroughly established that further reference to it would be like flogging a dead mule.

### THE IZRAILIES.

They are commonly called "Tàlees" because they are, throughout Western India, mainly engaged in oil (Tàle) pressing. As a matter of fact they are Jews, belonging, it is supposed, to the "lost tribe of Izrael" who, somehow, found their way first to Côchin on the Malabar coast, and then spread over the country. There is a tolerably large community of them in the City of Poona, who do not by

THE TÀLEE.

any means confine themselves to oil pressing, but are good mechanics, carpenters and artificers of all kinds. Many Tálees or Jews are in the army, many also are in the Police, where such men as the late Abraham David of the Ahmednuggur Police did rare good work. The more there are in the Police or. for the matter of that, in Government Service, the better for the State.

### THE GÔANESE (PORTUGUESE HALF-CASTES) AND OTHER EURASIANS.

There is a large Gôanese Community, harmless, indolent people not remarkable for abstention from strong drinks, breeders of poultry of all kinds, and pork; most of them are musicians, and many are in the native regimental bands. Some are petty shopkeepers, bakers and confectioners, many more are domestic servants, a few are carpenters and machinists. All are devout Roman Catholics; they have no sort of sympathy with the Bráhmins, who despise them. They have all the weakness of character of both the races from whom they are descended, vanity, love of dress, loquacity; like most mixed Eastern races, they are deficient in physique and perhaps in courage.

The other Eurasians of the present day resemble them in many ways, but the older families often contain fine specimens of the human race, possessed of much energy and endowed with courage. They join the Volunteer Corps, and would no doubt be staunch in action.

# CHAPTER XIX.

## THE POONA POLICE.

In the present troubles the Poona Police have been conspicuous not only for doing nothing, but for having, as a body, sedulously withheld from their superiors all information regarding the seditious conspiracy that has notoriously been working almost openly in the City. There cannot be a shadow of doubt that not a few of the City Police were privy to the Jubilee crimes to the extent that they knew that certain persons were banded together to commit some bloodthirsty outrage that should make the denizens of Government House quake in their shoes. There are, unquestionably, men in the Force who could at any moment have revealed the plot and pointed out the criminals, but it has been made much better worth their while to hold their tongues, especially as the Government, with fatuous imbecility, followed up its offer of an excessive reward by a second proclamation particularly stipulating that the Police shall not share in it!

In the 26th Chapter of my "Reminiscences of an Indian Police Official" (1894), I described the Police of the Western Presidency as follows.

"Of all sorts, sizes, and heights, the men present the appearance of a collection of shambling scarecrows. They are willing (as I have shown) and fairly honest, but fifty per cent of them, or more, are illiterate. Their antecedents are not usually bad (it is true), and many of them strike

POONA POLICE.

out to the front, and earn their small pensions meritoriously. But oh! they are so miserably paid! Horse-keeper—gardener—cow-men—the very cooly, or labourer, who works by the day—turns up his nose at the pittance the blue-coat Policeman receives. He is respected, because he is a man clothed (literally) in authority, but it is certain that he uses this authority in many petty ways to eke out his slender means."

On page 276 I pointed out that the deficiencies of the Police "cannot be supplied, and that their general *morale* can never be improved till they are sufficiently paid." Again, at page 278, I observed "The inevitable question will be asked—'Why should these things be?' 'Are there not District Magistrates and Commissioners to point out the need of reform, and to suggest a remedy?' The answer is, that these officers, for many years past, have never ceased pressing the question of police reform on reluctant Governments. The pigeon-holes of the Secretariats must be full of printed and unprinted matter on the subject. Secretaries to Government must have written reams, clerks must have compiled hundredweights of 'précis', and Honourable Members of Honourable Boards must have racked their brains in writing lucid Minutes on Police Reform. Lest I should be accused of exaggeration, I may mention, after counting each time, that the papers I alluded to—ignoring all that had passed before—began on the 22nd November, 1888, and terminated on 3rd February, 1894, thus covering five years and three months. The papers laid on the Editor's table (see the "Mahratta" of 18th February) enumerate seventeen letters, two telegrams, and four resolutions. Heaven only knows how many memos. and cross-memos, must have passed besides!"

To the second inevitable question—"Why, then, has nothing been done?"—I explained (p. 281), "The question of

Police Reform, like a hundred questions of more or less importance, has been from time to time shelved, to make room for whatever at the moment seemed the more pressing matter of the day. Famines, and kindred calamities, have stood in its way. Irrigation Works; Famine Relief Railways and their Feeders; Education, the great cormorant—with its technical and other greedy progeny; all these have come from time to time—most unrighteously—in the way of Police Reform, in truth, the greatest, the most important of them all.

"But Governors want to make their mark, not so much in India as in England, where their career, if they are ever to have any career, will be. They have a short term of office, and at least the first half of it is occupied in learning some smattering of the people they are governing. Pageants and tours take up a great deal of time, and they are naturally wary of indentifying themselves with reforms which they think will have only local bearing, and not tell effectively in their gubernatorial career as a whole.

"Thus has the question of Police Reform been systematically 'shunted', though several Governments, including Bombay, are understood to be strenuously striving to set their houses in order. It is a matter, moreover, which unquestionably involves increased expenditure; and for many years past, with the rupee steadily falling in value, there has been little to spare: no Governor would have dared to propose a substantial advance for Police purposes. Sir

Richard Temple—who has done more for Western India than can be accounted in millions sterling in the one matter of Forest organisation—would certainly have brought Police Reform to the front had he but stayed. But there are not many Indian Administrators possessed of Sir Richard's energy and experience."

Since my work was published—in fact while it was in the Press—a Bombay Police Reform Scheme was sanctioned and "placed on the Editor's table". It showed a vigorous attempt by Lord Harris to right a great wrong, but, alas! the monetary difficulty was against him! The pay of the Armed Police has been left untouched. A dangerous experiment has been tried with unarmed police on comparatively high pay. I need not indicate to any Anglo-Indian who has worked outside the Secretariat, what that has meant. Lord Harris's laudable but emasculated scheme now three years in operation, has evidently failed so far as Poona City is concerned.

There are other reasons for the failure in the City of the Peishwas. The cost of living there, for example, is perhaps double what it is elsewhere; the temptations are a hundredfold greater because the serious crimes of conspiracy, sedition, forgery and the like, are the inheritance of a certain wealthy clique who can well afford, not only to pay bribes and hush-money with lavish hands, but also to pay for the propagation of their peculiar patriotic programme.

Add to this that traditions of Gâssee Rám, Kôtwal or

Police Inspector of the City of Poona, under Bájee Rao the last Peishwa (1800), and of the infamous Trimbuckjee Dainglià, Bájee Rao's prime pimp and favourite, have not yet died out. No instance of greater neglect on the part of an administration, or of more extraordinary criminality in a subordinate officer, is recorded in the annals of any state than the case of Gâssee Rám, Kôtwal or Police Inspector of the City of Poona. This man, a Bráhmin native of Hindostan, "employed the power with which he was vested in perpetrating the most dreadful murders. People disappeared, and no trace of them could be found. Gâssee Rám was suspected, but Náná Furnáwees refused to listen to complaints, apparently absurd from their unexampled atrocity.

"At last, it being suspected that Gâssee Rám was starving a respectable Bráhmin to death, Mánnájee Phakray headed a party of the people, broke open the prison, and rescued the unfortunate Bráhmin, which led to the detection of the monster's crimes; and he fell a victim to the vengeance of the exasperated populace, by whom he was stoned to death. Trimbuckjee Dainglià was immediately appointed to the vacant office. Trimbuckjee was originally a jâsoos or spy, and brought himself to the Peishwa's notice when he fled to Mhár from the power of Hôlkar, by carrying a letter to Poona and bringing back a reply in a very short space of time. Being afterwards entertained on the personal establishment of the Peishwa, his activity, intelligence and vigour soon became conspicuous; and by unceasing diligence, and, above all, by being pander to his vices, never hesitating to fulfil his wishes whatever they might be, he gradually gained the confidence of his master, and was the only man who ever obtained it."

The Poona Police have often and often been more than suspected of torturing their prisoners; subornation of witnesses—"tutoring", as the Judges term it—has long been reduced to a science and studied in the "Scotland Yard" of Poona City, a spacious fortified palace in the very heart of the city, the only entrance by a well-guarded gateway, the Police Lines placed well away from the lock-ups, to which no one has access but the chief police officials and persons brought by them to interview the prisoners. Who can say how many captives have been, nay, even now may be subjected to cunning modes of torture which leave no trace? Who doubts—do not the records of fifty per cent of the Poona Sessions and the Magisterial cases prove it?—that in this hotbed of intrigue, false evidence? is systematically got up, and good evidence in weak cases bolstered up by bad?

As if all this was not bad enough, the personnel of the city Magistrates, the very office establishment of the Police Superintendent, aye! of the Commissioner of Police are in league. Any high official has only to indicate that a certain person is offensive to him, and a dead set is at once made against that unfortunate, who sooner or later will be "run in", or disgraced, or ruined.

The reform of the Poona City Police being now a measure

that must not be deferred, the direction which reform should take is simplicity itself.

The City contains 118,000 souls; it is encompassed by well-defined limits—the river, fortified gateways, and "nullahs" or water-courses banked with prickly pear surround it; the Military Cantonment—British and Native Regiments—lie within hail under its walls. *Ergo* no armed police are needed within the City; they dare not fire if firearms are needed, they would not fire if they dared.

It follows that the Police should be baton-armed constabulary and horse patrols (Sowárs) for the streets, with the reserve in Scotland Yard, with a carefully organised detective establishment selected from all classes, creeds and castes, whose names need not be published to the world. The Superintendent should reside in Scotland Yard—a salubrious, even a pleasant spot, where there is enough cut-stone lying loose to build him a little palace at small cost. Assistant to the Commissioner of Police *ex officio*, he should also have authority on emergency to communicate direct with His Excellency the Governor. His house should be connected by wire or telephone with Government House, the residences of the Commissioner of the Central Division, the Commissioner of Police and the Officer commanding at Poona. A secret code should be prepared by which he can communicate secretly by wire or letter to either of these high officials; this code should not be known to any other person. In a few years he would repay his cost by the detection and prevention of crime, not merely in

Poona, but all over India, for Poona City is the very navel of crime, the favourite resort of Hindoo criminals, as Bombay City is that of Mahommedans. He should be a picked man, as is the Commissioner of the Bombay Police —well paid and permanently appointed—*not* a youngster—*not* owing his promotion to mere seniority.

So shall the City of the Peishwas be efficiently policed and the Bráhmin cobra be scotched. Let the Secretary of State for India see to this; it is almost a matter of Imperial importance.

The cost can be easily provided. Let the Government grant in aid to Fergusson College be wholly withdrawn, let the grants for Deccan Higher Education generally be docked till the money needed is found. This will be more sensible, juster, and withal more practicable than imposing the cost of a Punitive Police Post on an innocent population.

# CHAPTER XX.

## SUMMARY AND CONCLUSION.

IT is plain from all that has preceded—from history, from traditions, from the writings of learned men from the earliest down to the latest days, from current events—that a spirit of general disaffection does not prevail in Máháráshtra, but is confined to a small body of evil-disposed persons belonging to an astute caste who, till British rule came, possessed all material power, wielded it for their own aggrandisement: who writhe now at the consciousness of having lost it by their treachery towards their rulers and themselves, while they strive, and will never cease to strive, to recover influence by any means, fair or foul.

Outside this caste, from the warlike Mahratta now fighting by our side, to the peasant and the petty trader, all Hindoos in the Western Presidency are, as in the nature of things they must be, well disposed towards the only Government that has ever given them security of life and property, that has ever reduced their burthens, fostered their trades, attempted to ameliorate their condition, that is even now labouring, as it has always, and will always labour, to mitigate the calamities of famine and pestilence.

And as to Mahommedans, they know full well that they owe their decadence, primarily, to Bráhmin influence and ambitious intrigues: secondarily, to their own apathy and indolence. Not a fragment of evidence has yet been adduced, or will ever be found, that there has been any connection between Bráhminical conspiracies and Mahommedan fanaticism, while there is abundant and recent proof, in the riots that have occurred throughout the land, of the mutual hostility between the "twice-born" and the followers of the Prophet. Mahommedans may not love us, may despise us for our fatuous folly in dealing with our real enemies, but they hate the Bráhmins with an intensity that cannot be gauged by European standards. They would join with alacrity in any measure likely to weaken Bráhminical influence, for they deplore, for their own sakes, the blind confidence with which we have played into the hands of the one sect against which history warns us.

The moral to be drawn is obvious; the course of wisdom is plain, if the powers that be will only pursue it. Let the caste in question be repressed not pampered. Let the public service be rendered more accessible for other castes and races, not kept well-nigh closed for all but Bráhmins.

No private person limits his cutlery to carving-knives, or replaces tried or well-worn blades by razors. That is what we have done, and so we have cut our fingers to the bone. Weaken Bráhminical influence by raising the status of the Mussulman; let the one counterpoise the other, but let neither party dominate. Look to the Educational Department; overhaul objectionable text books; withdraw or reduce grants for higher education, and devote the money to Mahommedan and lower-class schools and colleges. Watch the native Press vigilantly, and promptly punish seditious writings; the law has now been proved sufficient for its control without resort to insane suppression. Reform the Police from top to bottom and infuse therein the detective element it lacks. Try to rescue the peasantry from their indebtedness, and to extend irrigation by means that exist, without resorting to ambitious and costly schemes, which in most parts of Máháráshtra cannot be remunerative; resort rather to water-mining than to water-damming. Above all, govern Bombay, and Madras also, through experienced Lieutenant-Governors who know their India, not by placemen who have to learn its alphabet. Alas! this last and most essential of reforms is the most hopeless, for it touches patronage, which will doubtless continue to send out weak, ignorant, apathetic, or prancing proconsuls to the end of time..

FINIS.